Oxford
International
Resources

1

W0051271

Skills
Problem Solving and Reasoning

Karen Morrison
Lisa Greenstein

OXFORD
UNIVERSITY PRESS

OXFORD
UNIVERSITY PRESS

Great Clarendon Street, Oxford, OX2 6DP, United Kingdom

Oxford University Press is a department of the University of Oxford. It furthers the University's objective of excellence in research, scholarship, and education by publishing worldwide. Oxford is a registered trade mark of Oxford University Press in the UK and in certain other countries.

British Library Cataloguing in Publication Data
Data available

9781382044516

10 9 8 7 6 5 4 3 2

The manufacturing process conforms to the environmental regulations of the country of origin.

Printed in India by Multivista Global Pvt. Ltd

Acknowledgements
The publisher and authors would like to thank the members of our teacher panel for providing feedback on the materials:

Vaishali Arora; Ruth Evans; John Horsington MEAD, MEd; Sheetal Javeri; Gay Kidd; Joy Madzima; Sally Michel; Shanique Panton; George Papadimitriou; Gertrude Sackitey Badoe; Robyn Turner.

The publisher and authors would like to thank the following for permission to use photographs and other copyright material:

Photos: p31: Monkey Business Images / Shutterstock; **p38(t):** Ground Picture / Shutterstock; **p38, 39, 79(a):** freestore 839 / Shutterstock; **p42, 43:** Pogorelova Olga / Shutterstock; p43(t): UltraOrto, S.A./Shutterstock; **p43(b):** Oxford University Press; **p47:** Cozine / Shutterstock; **p50:** YummyBuum / Shutterstock; **p57(a):** ShotbyDSN / Shutterstock; **p57(b):** Lepas / Shutterstock; **p57(c):** Stsvirkun / Shutterstock; **p58(l):** Oxford University Press; **p58(r):** Lightspring / Shutterstock; **p62(a), 78(a):** Sari ONeal / Shutterstock; **p62(b), 78(b):** macropixel / 123RF; **p62(c), 78(c):** arka38 / Shutterstock; **p62(d), 78(d):** Thammanoon Khamchalee / Shutterstock; **p73:** Zadorozhnyi Viktor / Shutterstock; **p77(a):** 7th Son Studio / Shutterstock; **p77(b):** Siegfried Schenk / Shutterstock; **p77(c, d):** Resul Muslu / Shutterstock.

Cover art: Andrea Manzati.

Artwork by: Katya Balakina, Q2A Media and Oxford University Press.

Every effort has been made to contact copyright holders of material reproduced in this book. Any omissions will be rectified in subsequent printings if notice is given to the publisher.

This Student Book refers to the Cambridge Primary Mathematics framework published by Cambridge Assessment International Education. This work has been developed independently from and is not endorsed by or otherwise connected with Cambridge Assessment International Education.

The manufacturer's authorised representative in the EU for product safety is Oxford University Press España S.A. of el Parque Empresarial San Fernando de Henares, Avenida de Castilla, 2–28830 Madrid (www.oup.es/en).

Contents

My problem-solving record

These are the steps I follow to solve a problem...

1 Read and understand the problem → **2** Choose a strategy

These are the strategies I tried...

Act out the problem

① ② ③ ④ ⑤ ⑥

Use objects to model the problem

| 1 | 2 | 3 | 4 | 5 | 6 |

Draw a picture or a diagram

	9	
?	?	?

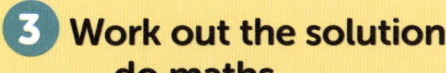

3 Work out the solution
  - do maths
  - show my work

4 Check my answers
  - compare with a partner

Look for patterns and make connections

2 → 4 → 6 → 8...

COUNT 2s

NEXT SHAPE IS

1	2
3	4
5	6

Make a list

2 ▲ S
3 ■ S
1 ●
2 ▬ S

✓
1
2
3
4
5
6

Use a table

△	✓ ✓
□	✓ ✓ ✓
○	✓
▬	✓ ✓

1	2	3	4	5	6

Each family is different. Some families are big, with many people. Some families are small.

My name is Layla. I live with my mum and my 4 brothers.

My name is Mohamed. I live with my 2 aunties, my granny and my 4 cousins.

My name is Sofia. I live with my 2 parents, 2 sisters and 2 brothers.

1 How many people live in each house? Write the number in the house.

Use small objects to count the people.

Sofia's house   Mohamed's house   Layla's house

Think, talk, write

2 Draw a line to match each sentence to the correct person.

My family has the most people.

My family has the fewest people.

My family has an odd number of people.

Layla

Mohamed

Sofia

3 The three children and their families go to a picnic together. How many people are there **altogether**?

Draw a picture to help you work it out.

_____ people

1 Layla and Sofia drew this **diagram** to show the letters in their names. Discuss with a partner.

> A diagram is a kind of picture. It helps us to show **information**.

   a What do you notice about the letters in the diagram?

   b How did Layla and Sofia decide where to write the letters? Draw a line to match each label to the correct part of the diagram.

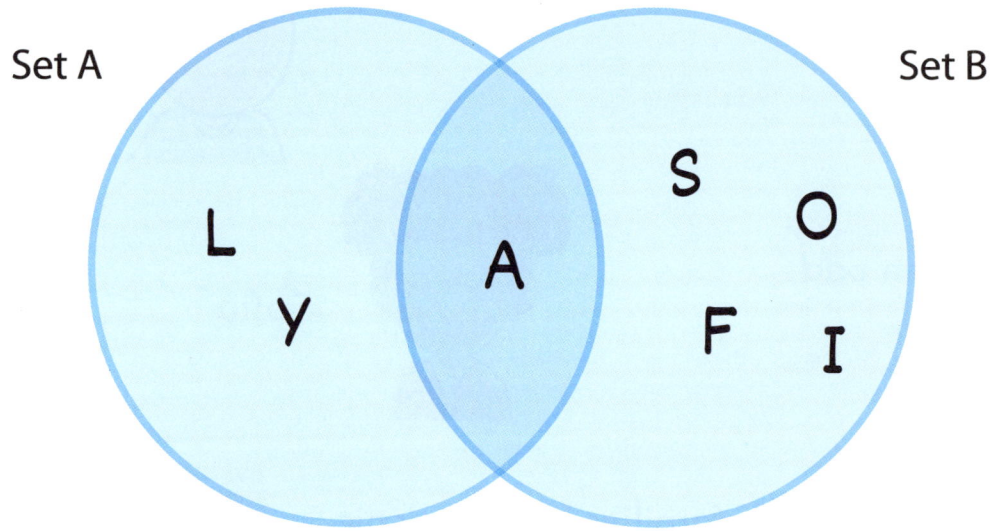

Set A   Set B

| Letters in both names | Letters in LAYLA but not in SOFIA | Letters in SOFIA but not in LAYLA |

2 Follow the instructions to complete the diagrams on page 9.

a Work with a partner. Complete a diagram to show the letters in your name and your partner's name.

_____

_____

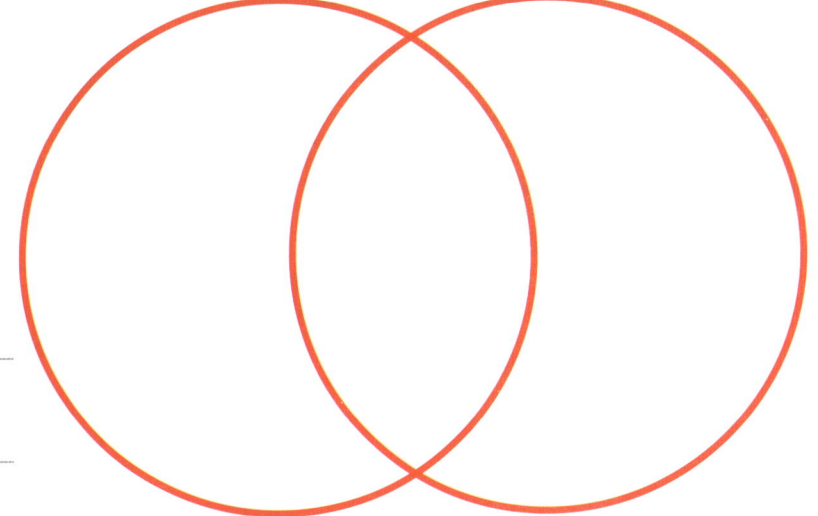

b Complete a diagram to show the letters in MAX and MOHAMED.

MAX

MOHAMED

c Choose two names from your family or from your class. Complete a diagram to show the letters in the two names.

_____

_____

Every year you get
1 year older. You add
1 year to your age.

1 Think of people
who are older and
younger than you.
Complete the
sentences in the boxes.

_____ is younger
than me.

They are _____ years old.

They are _____ years
younger than me.

_____ is older
than me.

They are _____ years old.

They are _____ years older
than me.

2 Someone born 1 year before you is 1 year older than you.
Work out the age of someone born:

a 2 years before you. _____ years old

b 5 years before you. _____ years old

3 Someone born after you is younger than you.
Work out the age of someone born:

a 2 years after you. _____ years old

b 4 years after you. _____ years old

Let's solve …

4 Mohamed's age is 6. The ages are missing from the other boxes.

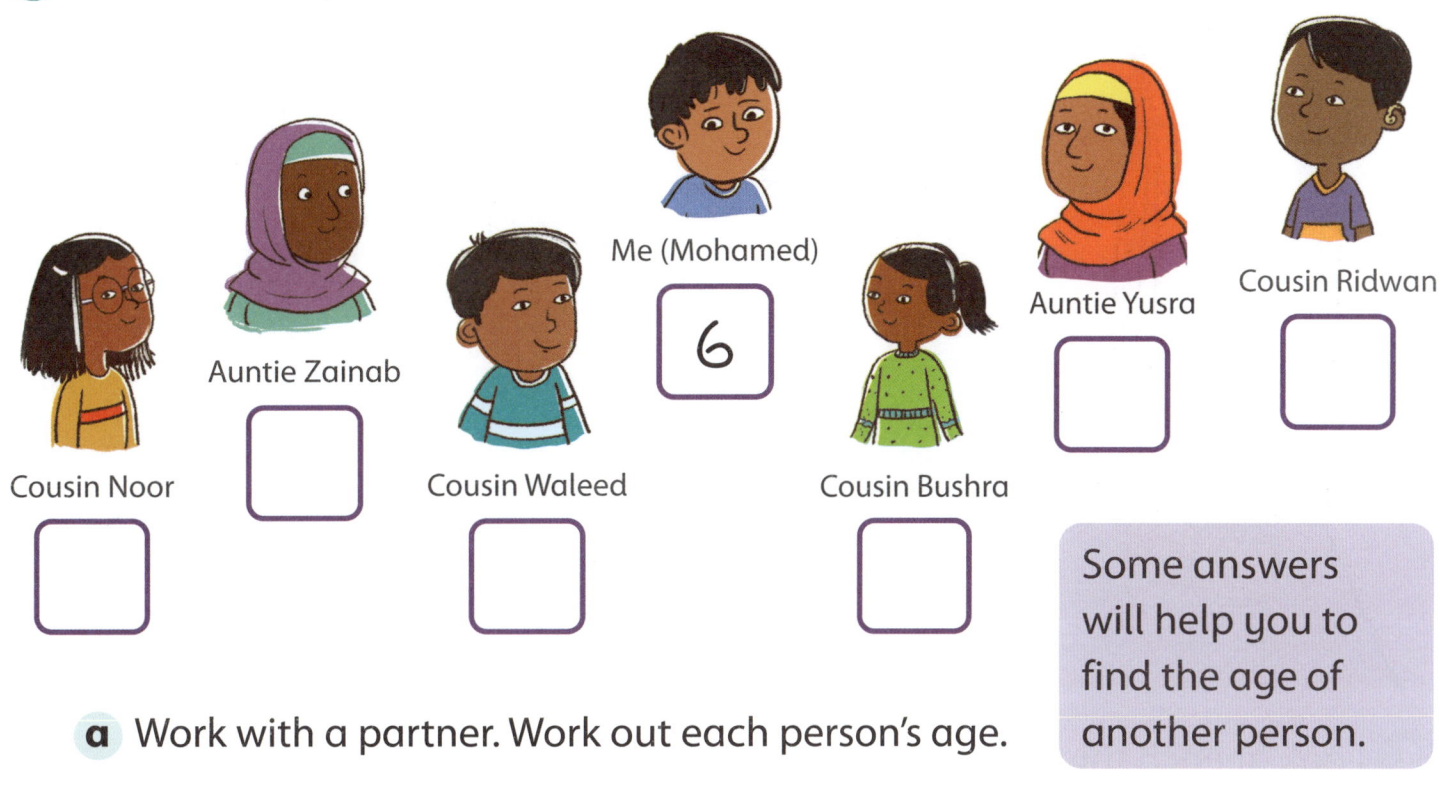

a Work with a partner. Work out each person's age.

> Some answers will help you to find the age of another person.

Auntie Zainab is 10 years older than Auntie Yusra.

Cousin Noor was born 7 years before me.

Auntie Yusra is 25 years older than me.

Cousin Waleed was born 4 years after Cousin Noor.

In 12 years, Cousin Ridwan will be 20.

Cousin Bushra is 3 years younger than me.

b How did you solve this problem? Tick ✓ the things you did.

I counted.	I used number facts.	I used objects.	I acted it out.	I drew a diagram.	I did something else.

This is the room that 3 of Layla's brothers **share**.

1 Look at each thing.
Count how many in the picture.

A pair is a group of 2.

a  _____ clock

b  _____ pillows

c  _____ seats

d  _____ **pairs** of shoes

e  _____ books

f  _____ wardrobes

2 Talk to a partner. Find different ways to complete each sentence.

a The number of pillows **equals** the number of _____.

b The number of wardrobes equals the number of _____.

Equals means is the same number.

12

Think, talk, write

3 **a** How many pairs of shoes does each brother have? Draw a picture or act it out.

> Remember, Layla has three brothers.

b Tell a partner how you worked it out. Does your partner have the same answer? Share your ideas.

4 Look at the rug on page 12. The pattern has three different shapes.

a Count each shape. Colour blocks in the **block diagram** to show how many.

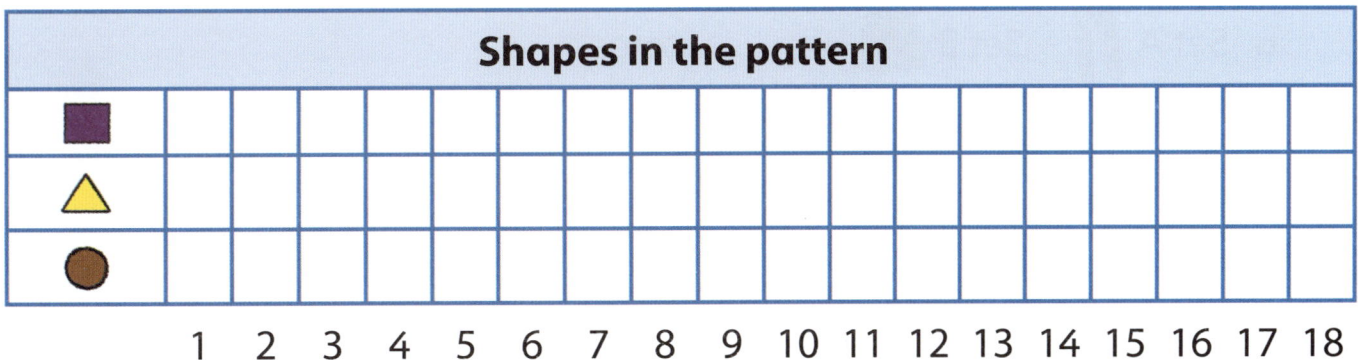

Shapes in the pattern

b Work with a partner. Complete the sentences.

There are _____ more △ than ■.

There is _____ more ■ than ●.

Mohamed is sorting his clothes into sets.

1 Count each type of clothing. Complete the block diagram.

Mohamed's clothes											
Set A Long pants											
Set B Shorts											
Set C T-shirts											
Set D Vests											

1 2 3 4 5 6 7 8 9 10

2 How many items altogether?

a Set A + Set B = _____ items

b Set C + Set D = _____ items

3 Mohamed buys some new clothes. How many must he add to make the total?

a Set B + _____ = 10 items

b _____ + Set D = 6 items

c Tell a partner how you worked it out.

Think, talk, write

4 Work with a partner. Read the story about the socks. Work out the missing numbers.

a There are _____ socks hanging on the line.

There are _____ pairs and _____ extra.

b Sofia puts all the blue striped socks in the basket.

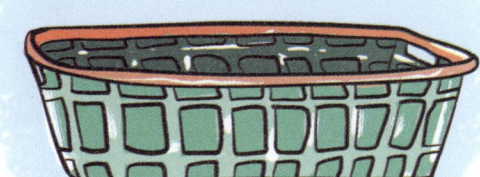

Now there are _____ socks on the line and _____ socks in the basket.

c Next, Sofia puts one pair of plain yellow socks in the basket.

Now there are _____ socks on the line and _____ socks in the basket.

d Then Sofia puts all the spotty socks in the basket.

Now there are _____ socks in the basket and _____ socks on the line.

5 Use the story to help you complete the table. The first line has been completed for you.

	Socks on the line	Socks in the basket	Subtraction
a	15	0	15 − 0 = 15
b			15 − _____ = _____
c			15 − _____ = _____
d			15 − _____ = _____

1 Layla asked some students to choose their favourite toy.
She gave them a list of toys to choose from.

Favourite toys		
Toy cars	🚗	🟢 🟢 🟢 🟢
Plushies	🐰	🟢 🟢 🟢 🟢 🟢 🟢 🟢
Dolls	👧	🟢 🟢 🟢 🟢
Bricks	🧱	🟢 🟢 🟢 🟢 🟢 🟢 🟢 🟢 🟢
Other toys	✈️🏐🥁	🟢 🟢 🟢 🟢 🟢

 = 1 student

a How many students chose toy cars? _____

b Which was the most **popular** toy?

> The most popular toy is the toy that most people like.

_____

c How many students did Layla ask altogether? Show how you work it out.

2 Layla puts the students into groups. How many students are in each group?

All the students who chose  or 🚗.

There are _____ students in this group altogether.

All the students who chose  or 🧱.

There are _____ students in this group altogether.

Layla likes to group her toy cars in different ways.

3 Layla groups the cars in pairs. How many pairs can she make? How many cars are left over?

_____ pairs _____ left over

4 Layla says:

> It doesn't matter how many cars you have. When you make pairs, you always have either one or zero left over.

Use different numbers of small objects to make pairs. Is Layla right? Share your ideas with your partner.

5 Now Layla puts the cars into 3 teams: A, B and C. She follows these rules.

> Use all 13 cars. Team A and Team B must have an equal number of cars. Team C can have any number of cars.

Layla makes these teams:

A	A	A	A	B	B	B	B	C	C	C	C	C

Team A has 4 cars. Team B has 4 cars. Team C has 5 cars.
4 + 4 + 5 = 13

Show another way to make the teams. Follow the same rules.

Team A has _____ cars. Team B has _____ cars. Team C has _____ cars.

_____ + _____ + _____ = _____

Turn back to page 4 and complete the problem-solving record.

2 Clean and tidy

Wash your hands!

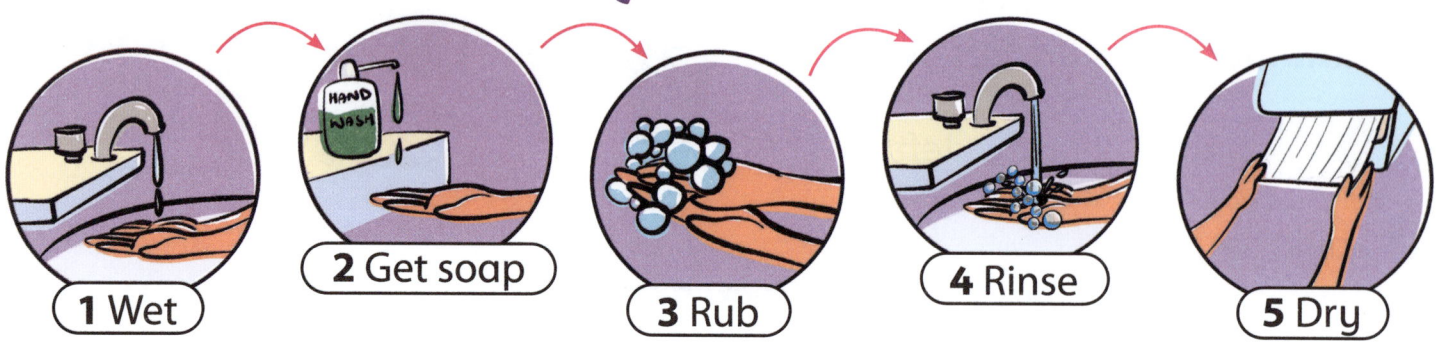

1 Wet **2 Get soap** **3 Rub** **4 Rinse** **5 Dry**

1 Answer these questions in your group.

   a Why do we wash our hands?

   b When should we wash our hands?

   c How do you wash your hands? Show your partner.

2 Look at the pictures.

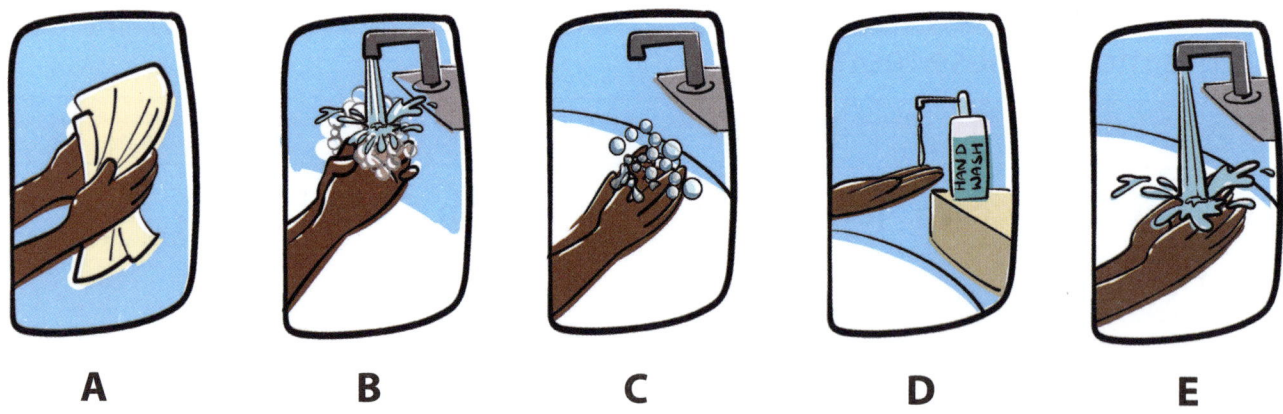

  A   **B**   **C**   **D**   **E**

Write the letters in the boxes to show the correct order for washing your hands.

First	Next	Then	After that	Last

Think, talk, write

3 How well do we wash our hands?

Listen to your teacher.

Tick ✓ true or false.

a We forget to wash the tips of our fingers often.

True ☐ False ☐

b We wash between our fingers very well.

True ☐ False ☐

c The backs of our thumbs are very clean.

True ☐ False ☐

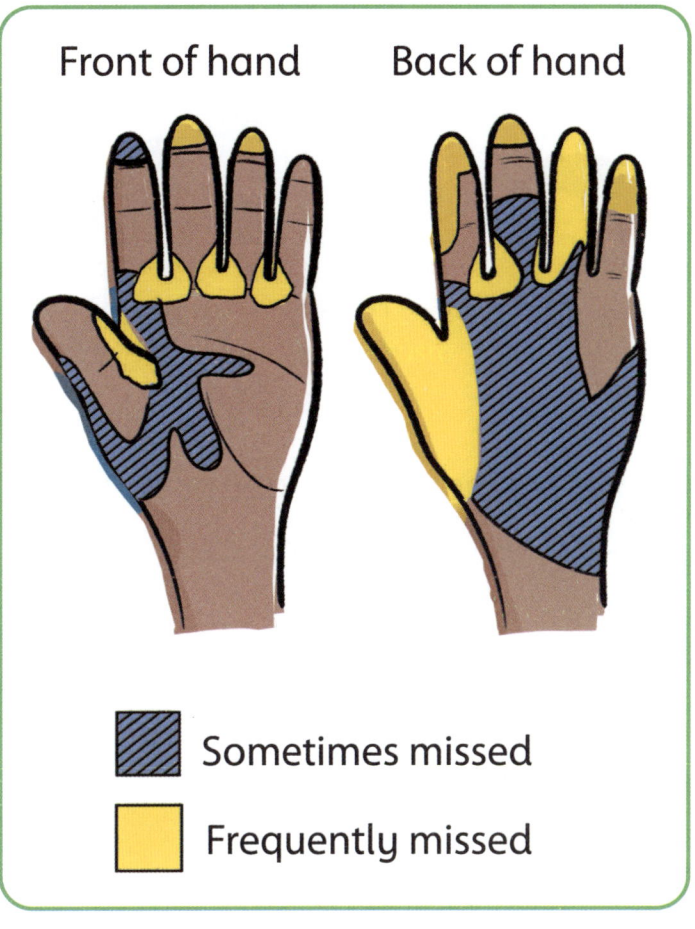

Front of hand   Back of hand

▨ Sometimes missed

▨ (yellow) Frequently missed

4 Which things clean your hands best?

Tick ✓ boxes in the table to show your answer.

	With soap	**Without soap**
With water		
Without water		

1 Zola has a cold. When he sneezes, germs move from his nose to his hands. Talk about how germs spread from Zola to other students.

2 Germs make more germs very quickly. Look at this picture.

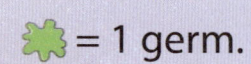 = 1 germ.

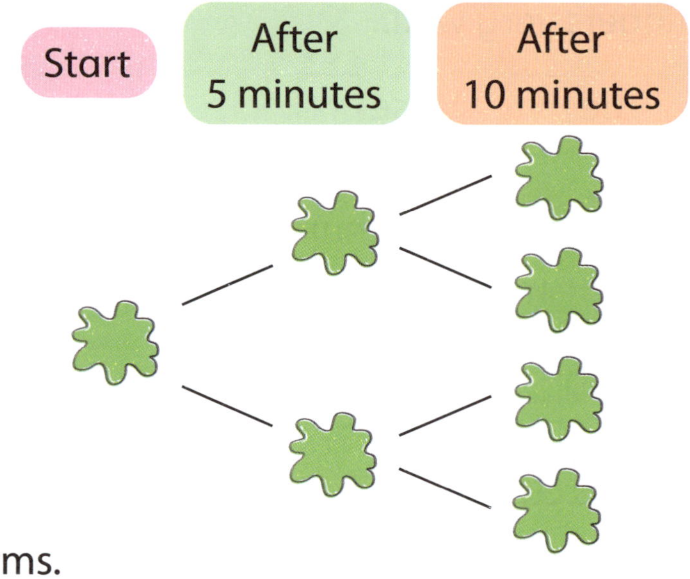

| Start | After 5 minutes | After 10 minutes |

a Write the number of germs.

How many germs?	1		

b Tick ✓ true or false.

- The number of germs **doubles** every 5 minutes.   True ☐   False ☐

- After 5 minutes there are 4 germs.   True ☐   False ☐

- After 15 minutes there will be 8 germs.   True ☐   False ☐

3 A different germ makes new germs like this.

Start   2 minutes   4 minutes   6 minutes   8 minutes

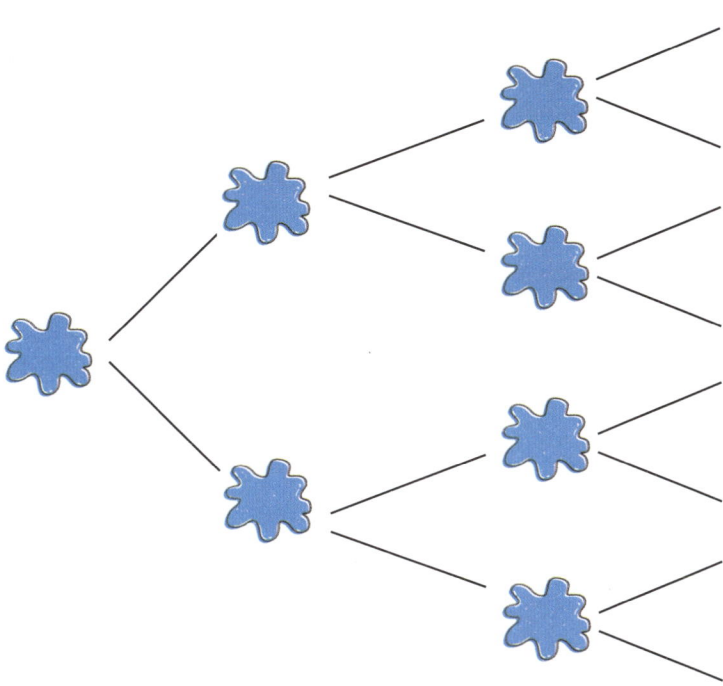

How many germs?

1	2			

a Draw the germs after 6 minutes.

b Write the number of germs at each time.

c How many germs will there be after 8 minutes? _____

d How did you work this out? Tick ✓ the things you did.

I drew the germs. ☐	I used number patterns. ☐	I doubled the number. ☐	I did something else. ☐

Think, talk, write

1 Look at the picture.
What do you see?

Count the items and write the numbers.

- I counted _____ bins.

- _____ bins are outside. _____ bin is inside.

- I counted _____ pieces of litter on the ground.

2 Mia sees 5 cans near the bin. She picks up 3 cans.

How many are left? _____ cans.

3 On day 1, there are 4 chip packets on the ground.
On day 2, there are 2 more. On day 3, there is 1 more.

day 1   day 2   day 3

How many are there on day 3? _____ chip packets.

Let's solve ...

4 What is it made of? Use different colours to match the litter to the correct bin. Two have been done for you.

5 There are five bags of garbage outside.

Work out the missing numbers.

a 2 bags are full. _____ are not full.

b 1 bag is heavy. _____ bags are not heavy.

c 3 bags have holes. _____ bags do not have holes.

d 4 bags fit in the bin. _____ bag is too big to fit in the bin.

6 Tell your group how you worked out the missing numbers.

Think, talk, write

Class 1 picked up litter in the school yard after lunch. They used stickers to make this **chart**.

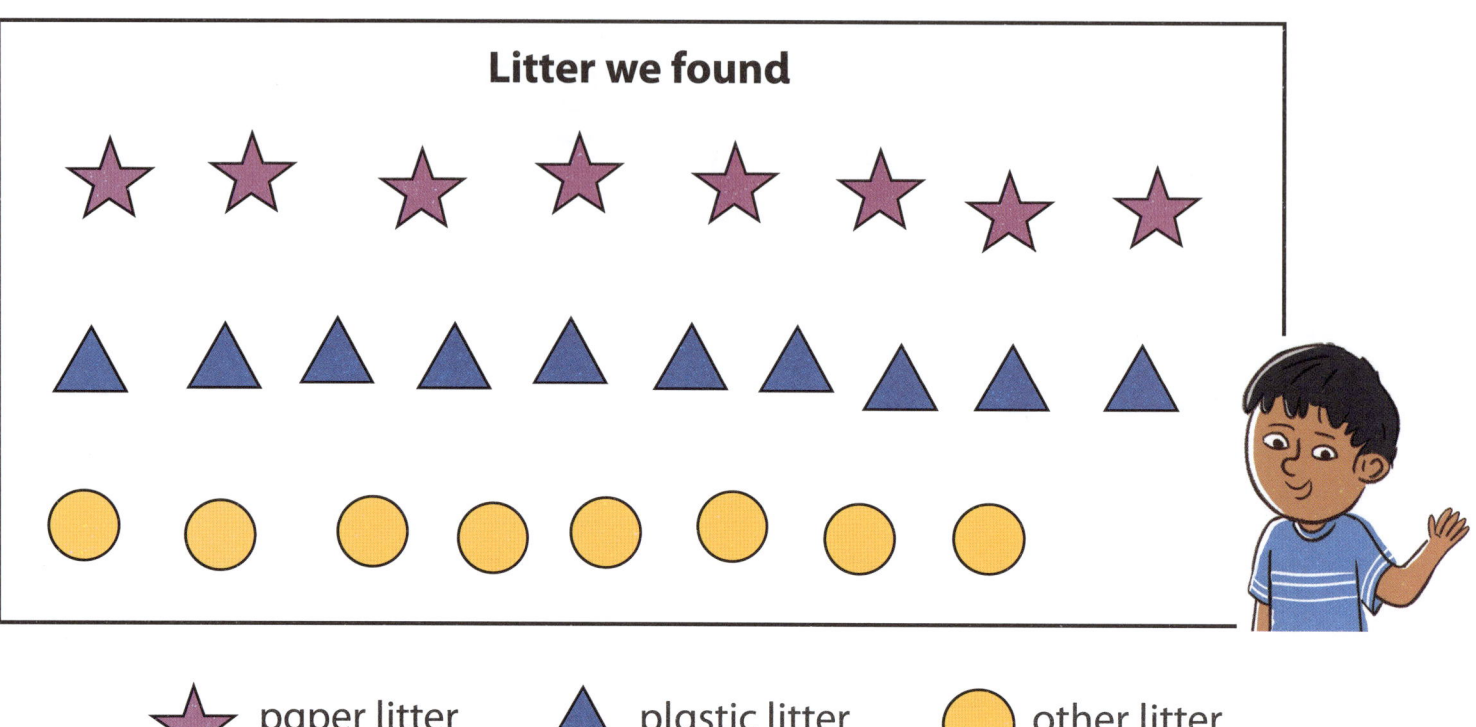

Litter we found

★ paper litter   ▲ plastic litter   ● other litter

1 Talk about the chart with a partner.

- What does the chart show? How do you know this?
- What do you think each sticker means? Why?
- How many types of litter did the students pick up?
- How many pieces of paper did they pick up?

2 The students found most of the litter near the tuck shop.

- Why do you think this is?
- What could the school do to solve this problem? Share your ideas with the class.

3 Misha used the information on the chart to make this table.

a Write numbers to finish the table.

Type of litter	Number of pieces of litter
Paper	
Plastic	
Other	

b Colour blocks in the block diagram to show this **data**.

Type of litter

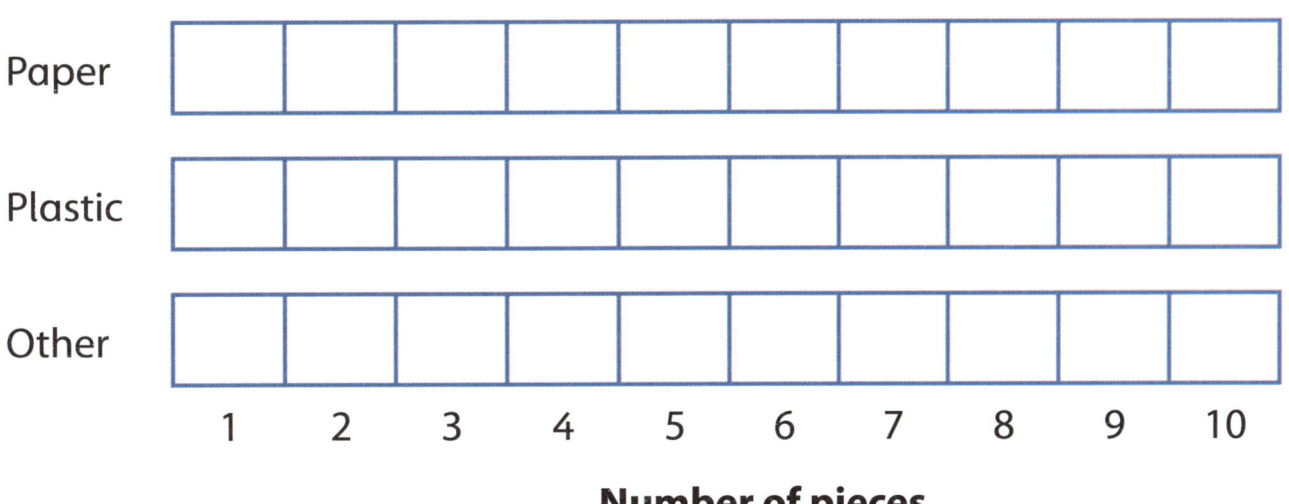

Number of pieces

4 Choose the correct word in each sentence. Trace the word.

a There is more / less paper than plastic.

b There are eight / nine pieces of paper.

c There is an equal number of pieces of paper and plastic / other litter.

Think, talk, write

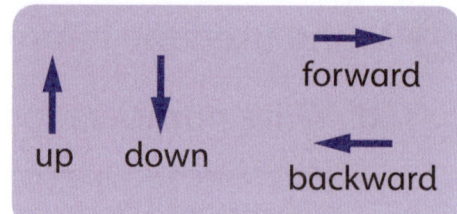

1 Here are two different paths that Li can walk to the recycling bin.

a Fill in the missing numbers for path B.

A

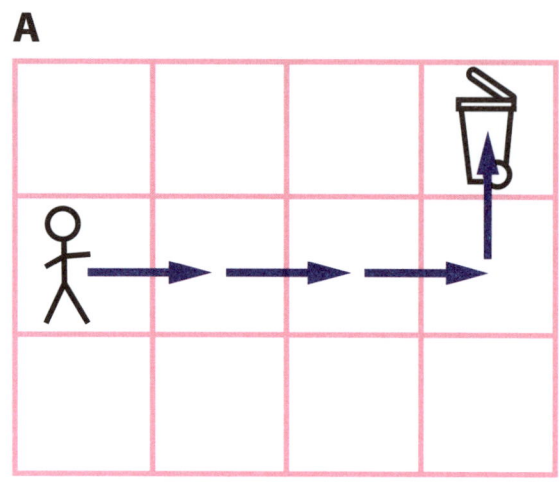

B

3 blocks forward

1 block up

_____ block down

_____ blocks forward

_____ blocks up

b Draw this path on the **grid**.

1 block forward

1 block up

2 blocks forward

Let's solve …

2 Kofi used a stick to draw circle tracks around the bin.

- Each track is 1 stick wide.
- He counted the pieces of litter in each track.
- He drew a table and a diagram to show how many.

How can you complete the table and the diagram so they match?

How far is the litter from the bin?

Distance from the bin	Number of pieces of litter
1 stick	9
2 sticks	10
3 sticks	
4 sticks	7

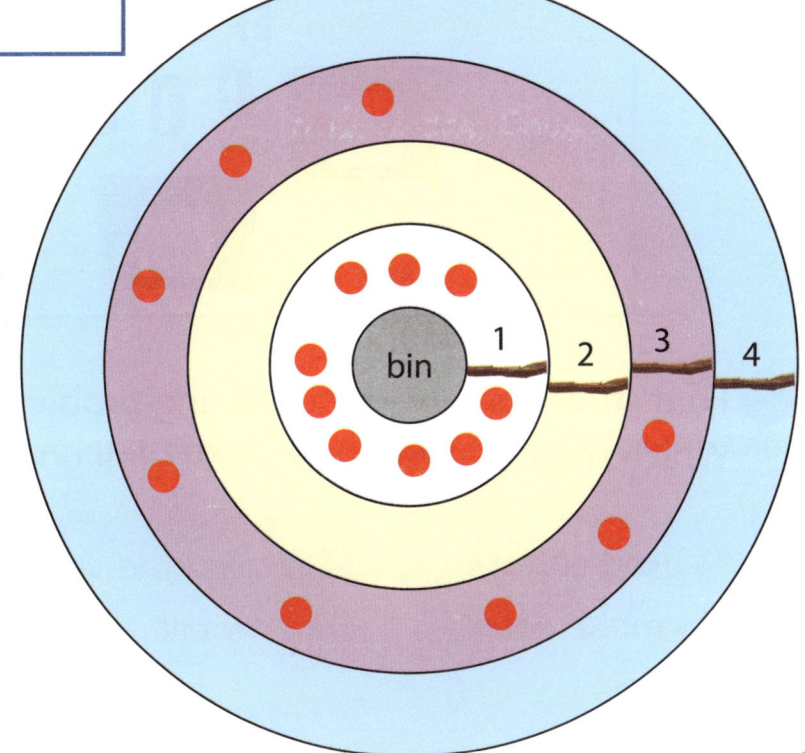

Let's solve …

1 Put an equal number of cans into each recycling bin.
Write the number in each bin.

a

b

c

d

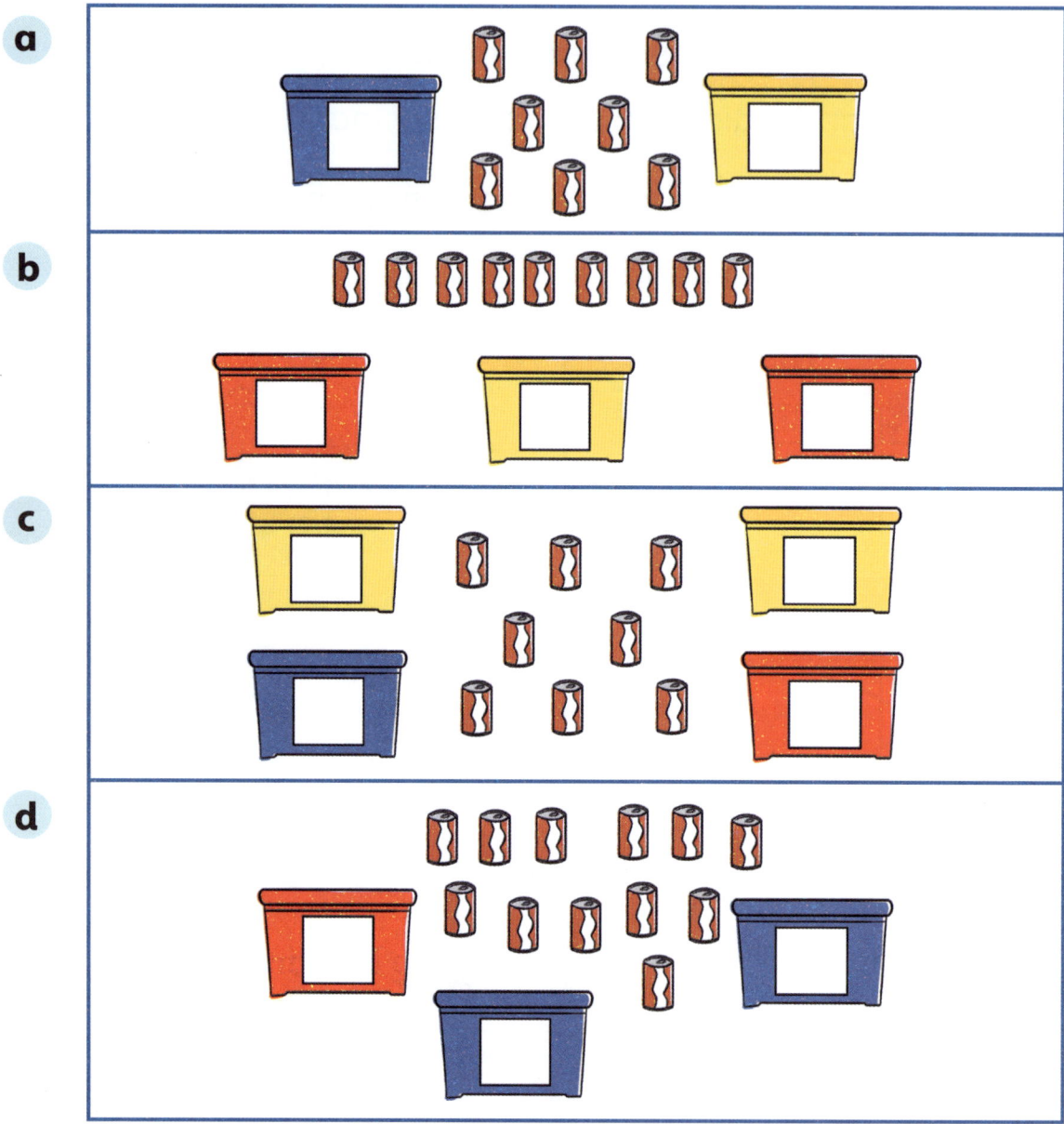

2 Four students solved the sharing problems. Read what they did.
Which method do you like best? Tell your group why.

I used objects to make equal groups.

I shared the cans one by one.

I drew dots and crossed out cans.

I shared in groups.

3 The garbage truck visits each house once to collect the garbage.

  a Draw a route for the truck. The truck must visit each house only once.

  b Compare your routes in your group. Tell each other how you made your routes.

How can you model this problem to help you solve it?

 4 Michelle puts 3 glass bottles in the recycling bin each day.

  a How many days will it take to put 9 bottles in the bin?

  _____

  b How many days will it take to put 15 bottles in the bin?

  _____

  → Turn back to page 4 and complete the problem-solving record.

1 Jay walks to Malik's house. They walk together to school.

Jay's house

School

- Where does Malik live? How did you work it out?

- Follow the route to school with your finger. Say what Jay and Malik pass on the way.

- One day Jay walks to school without Malik. Draw the shortest route from Jay's house to school.

2 This **pictogram** shows how the other students in Jay and Malik's class travel to school.

a Draw faces on the pictogram for Jay and Malik.

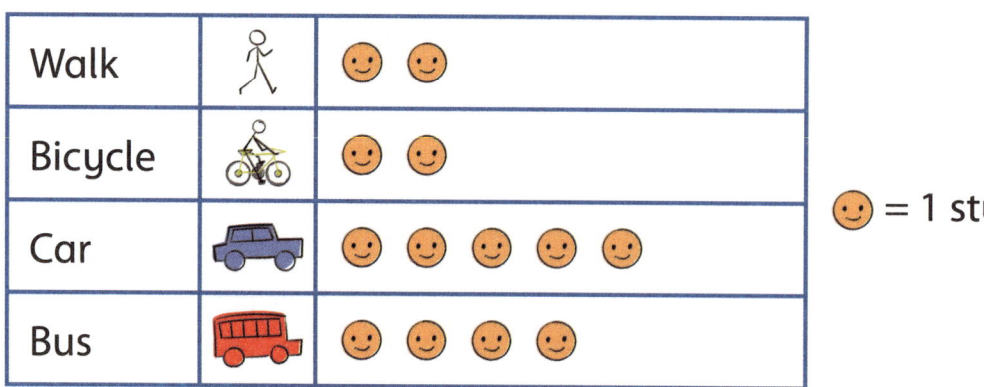

= 1 student

b Talk about the pictogram with a partner. What does it show?

Let's solve …

3 Read this problem.

- At Stop A, 2 students get on the bus.
- At Stop B, 1 student gets on.
- At Stop C, 2 students get on and 1 student gets off.
- At Stop D, 1 student gets on and 2 students get off.

How many students are on the bus now?

a Act out the problem.

b Here are four ways that students solved the problem.

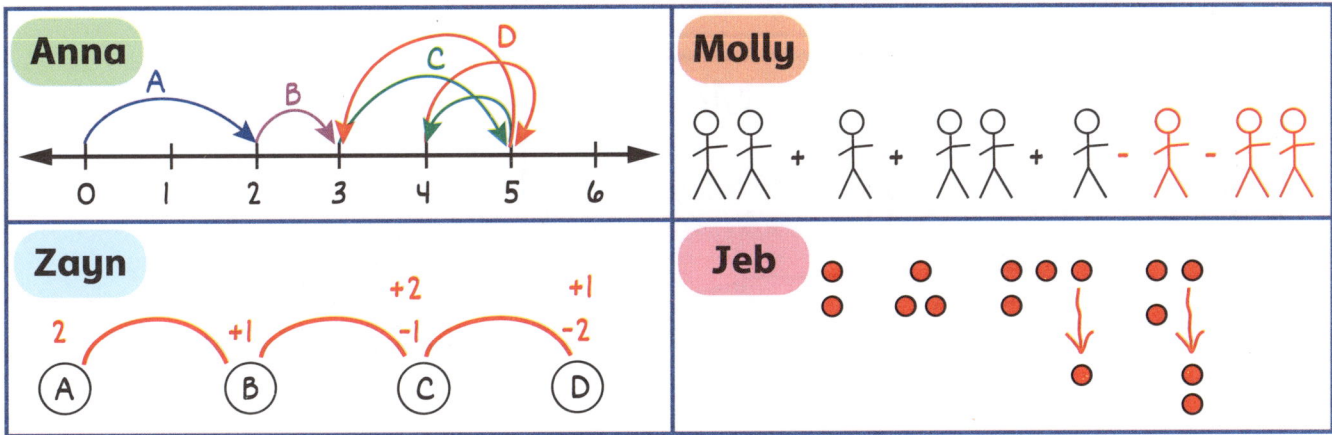

- What did each student do?
- Which way do you like best? Why?

c Try to show another way to solve the problem.

Think, talk, write

1 Whose locker is it?

Read the **clues**. Circle the correct name.

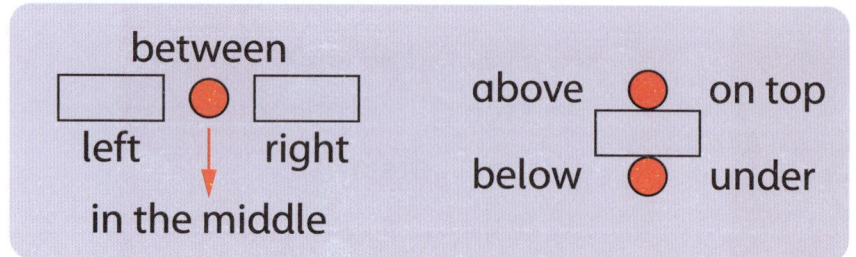

a	At the top, to the left of Mae's locker.	Zef	Ani
b	At the bottom in the middle.	Mae	Mo
c	At the top, above Neo's locker.	Mae	Zef
d	On the bottom, to the left of Mo's locker.	Kofi	Neo

2 Make up your own clue for a locker.
Ask your partner whose locker it is.

Let's solve ...

3 Five students are waiting in a line.

a Read the clues and write the students' names.

> Bem is behind Enzo. There is no one between them.

> Diego is between Cal and Enzo.

> Cal is behind Abay.

_____ _____ _____ _____ _____

b Who is first in line? _____

c How can you act out this problem to solve it?
Try your ideas in a group.

d Mira makes these five cards with the letters A, B, C, D and E.

- How can she use these to work out the names?

- Try this yourself.

| A | B | C | D | E |

Think, talk, write

1 Trace the words to write the name of each shape.

rectangle   circle   square

- Draw a line on each shape to make two halves.
- What new shapes did you make? Tell a partner.

2 Colour the shape that does not belong in each set.
Tell your partner why it does not belong.

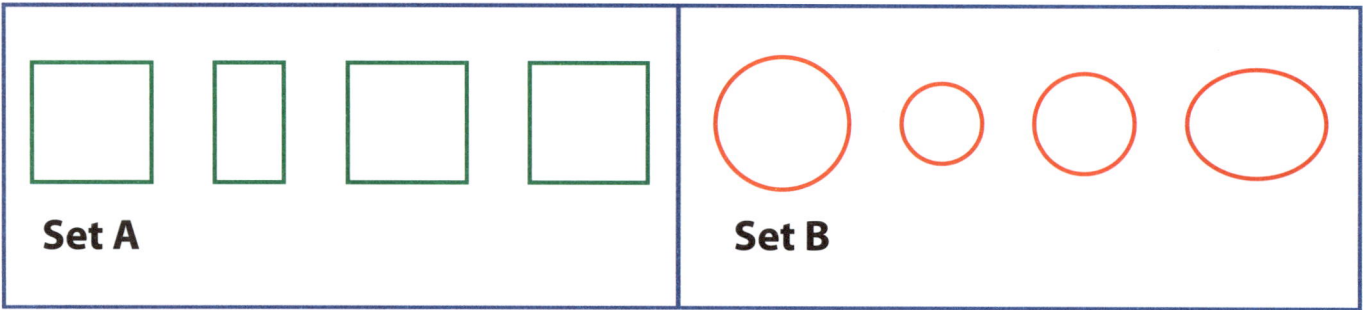

Set A   Set B

3 Look at this **plan** of a netball court.

a How many circles can you find?

b How many rectangles can you find?

c What shape do you make if you put B and C together?

_____

A plan is a diagram of a place looking from above.

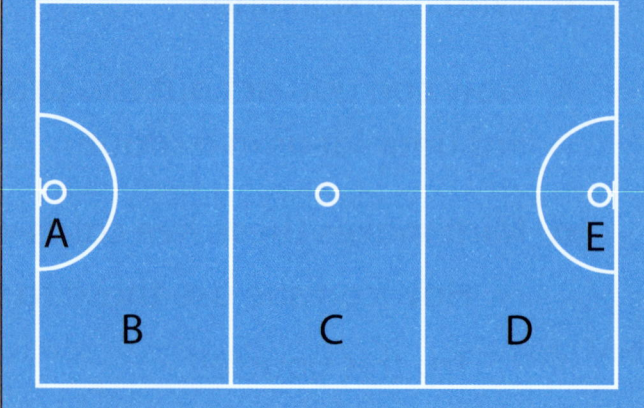

Let's solve …

4 This is a plan of a soccer field.

a How many circles can you make with the parts of circles on the field?

b Pedro walks around the field from A to B to C. Lionel walks across the field from A to C.

- Who walks further?

  _____

- Prove to your partner that your answer is correct.

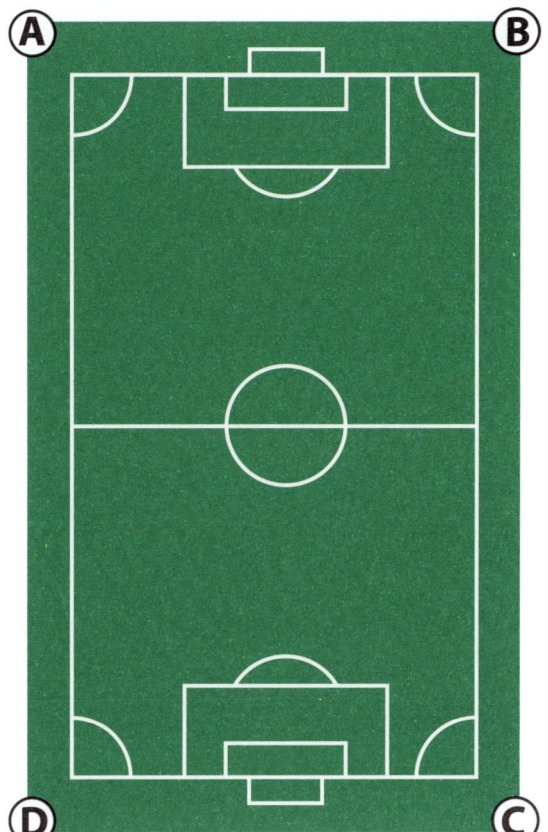

5 There are 11 players in a soccer team.

Write the missing numbers.

a There is 1 goalkeeper and _____ other players.

b There are 4 defenders and _____ other players.

c There are 2 forwards, 4 midfielders and _____ other players.

Let's reason ...

1 Talk about this plan of a classroom.

- What do you see in the classroom?
- What questions do you have?

2 These objects are all shown on the plan.

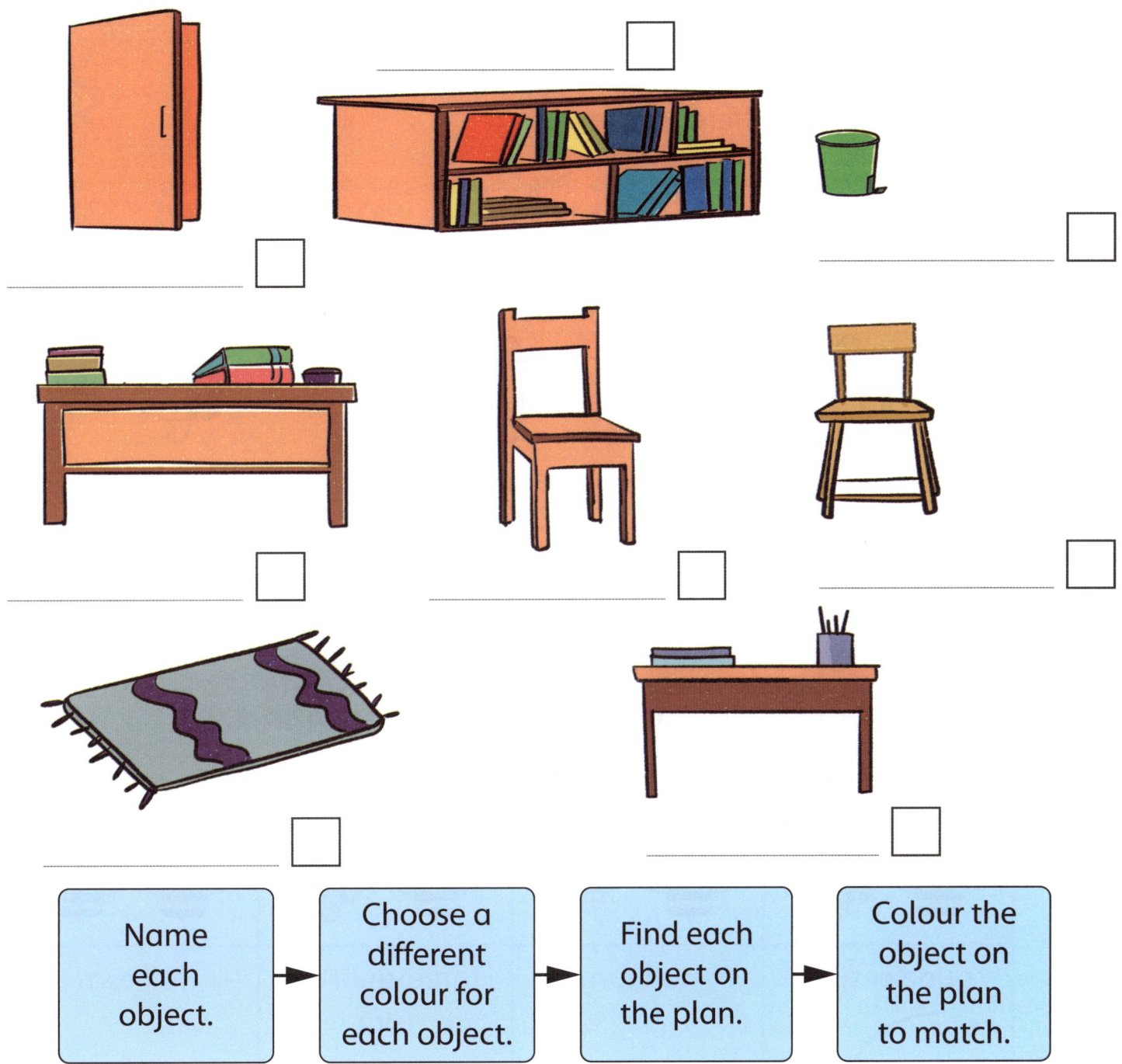

| Name each object. | → | Choose a different colour for each object. | → | Find each object on the plan. | → | Colour the object on the plan to match. |

3 Tell your partner how you found the objects on the plan.

4 The teacher needs to add 4 more chairs.

- Draw where she should put them.

- Tell your partner why you put the chairs there.

Think, talk, write

Lee is learning to code.

She uses a computer to move a small robot bee.

1 Lee has to know the difference between left and right.

a Is the bee facing left or right? Circle the correct answer.

left right	left right	left right

b How do you remember the difference between left and right? Tell your partner.

2 Lee must tell the bee how to **turn**. It can turn in four ways.

a Draw arrows to show each turn. The first one is done for you.

quarter turn	half turn	three-quarter turn	full turn

b Use a real object. Make each turn.

Let's solve ...

3 Match the bees to the turns.

> A bee can turn to the right (clockwise) or left (anti-clockwise).

quarter turn   half turn   full turn

4 Follow Lee's instructions. Draw the bee in its end **position**.
Use the arrows you drew on page 38 to help you.

start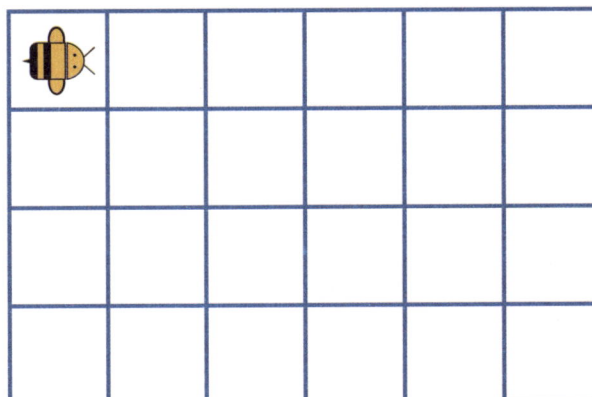

- 3 right then a quarter turn
- 2 down then a quarter turn
- 1 left then a half turn
- 3 right then a three-quarter turn

5 Work with a partner. The pictures show the bee's start and end positions.

a Write or draw two different sets of directions to turn the bee.

start  end

b Share your ideas in a group. How many different answers do you have?

Let's reason ...

1 There are 3 groups of students in a class.
The teacher shares the counters and shapes equally between the groups.

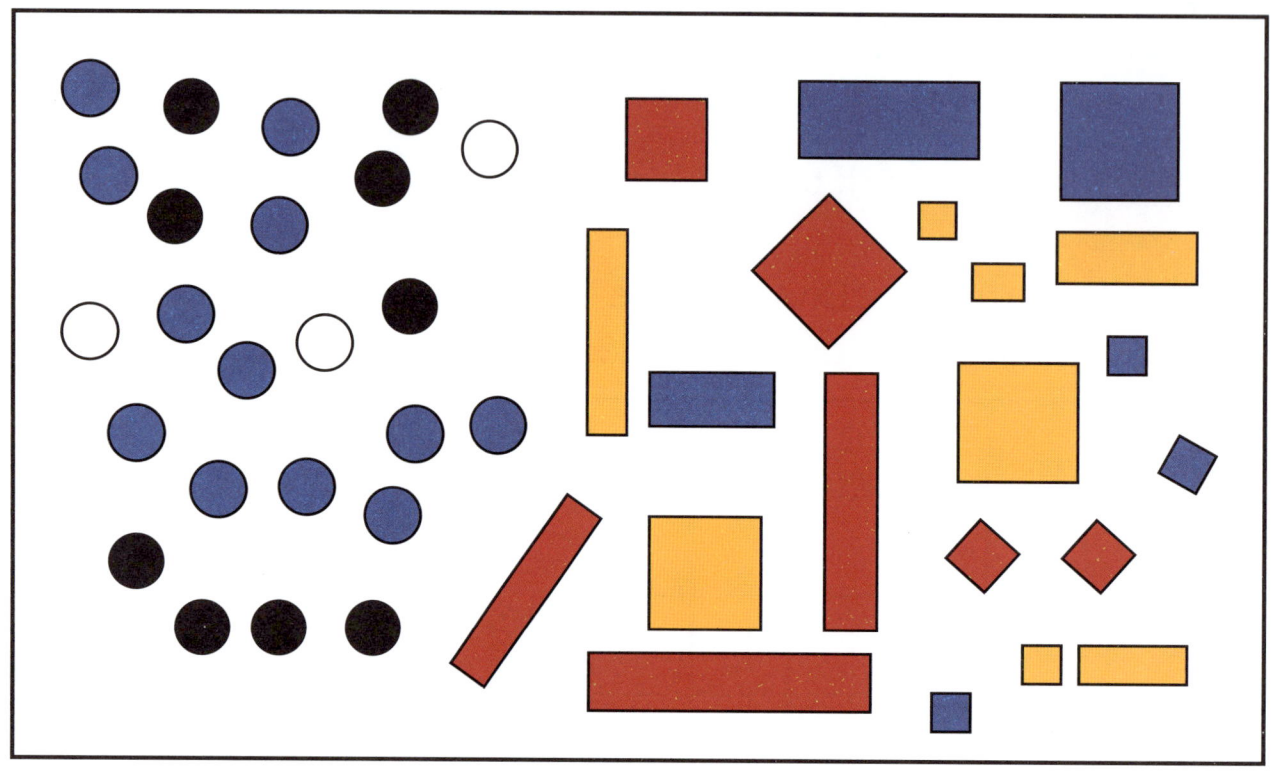

a Share the counters and shapes.

b How many should each group get?

blue counters	squares	black counters

white counters	green counters	rectangles

c How did you solve this problem? Tick ✓ the things you did.

I used objects to model the problem.	I drew the counters and shapes.	I counted in ones.	I counted in groups.	I did something else.

Let's solve ...

2 There are 2 students at each desk.
How many students are there at 5 desks?
Complete the table.

Number of desks	1	2	3	4	5
Number of students					

3 There are 4 students in a group.
How many students are there in 5 groups?

4 Malik puts crayons into pots.

- There are 30 pots.

- He puts a blue crayon in every third pot.

- He puts a yellow crayon in every fourth pot.

- He puts a black crayon in every fifth pot.

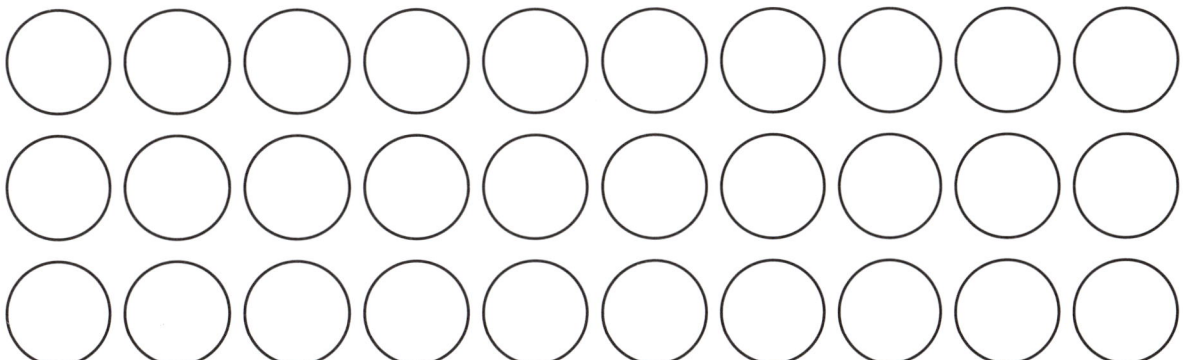

How many pots will have 2 crayons in them? ☐ pots
Colour the pots with 2 crayons.

➡ Turn back to page 4 and complete the problem-solving record.

In hopscotch, players hop and jump along the track. They start at 1 and hop on all the numbers to 10.

1 Use position words to describe the positions of the numbers.

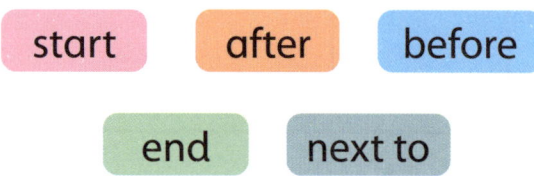

start　　after　　before

end　　next to

a 10 is at the _____ and

1 is at the _____ .

b 2 is _____ 3 and

5 is _____ 6.

c 7 is _____ 9

and _____ 5.

2 Some numbers are in pairs. The **sum** of the first pair is 5.
2 + 3 = 5
Find the sum of:

The sum is the total when you add numbers.

a the middle pair _____

b the last pair. _____

Let's solve …

3 Work with a partner. Write the hopscotch numbers in a different order. Follow these rules.

- The smallest number is at the end.

- The greatest number is at the start.

- The sum of the last pair is 6. The smaller number is before the greater number.

- The sum of the middle pair is 17. The greater number is first.

- There are no even numbers in the second or third **row**.

- The sum of the first pair is 10. The smaller number is first.

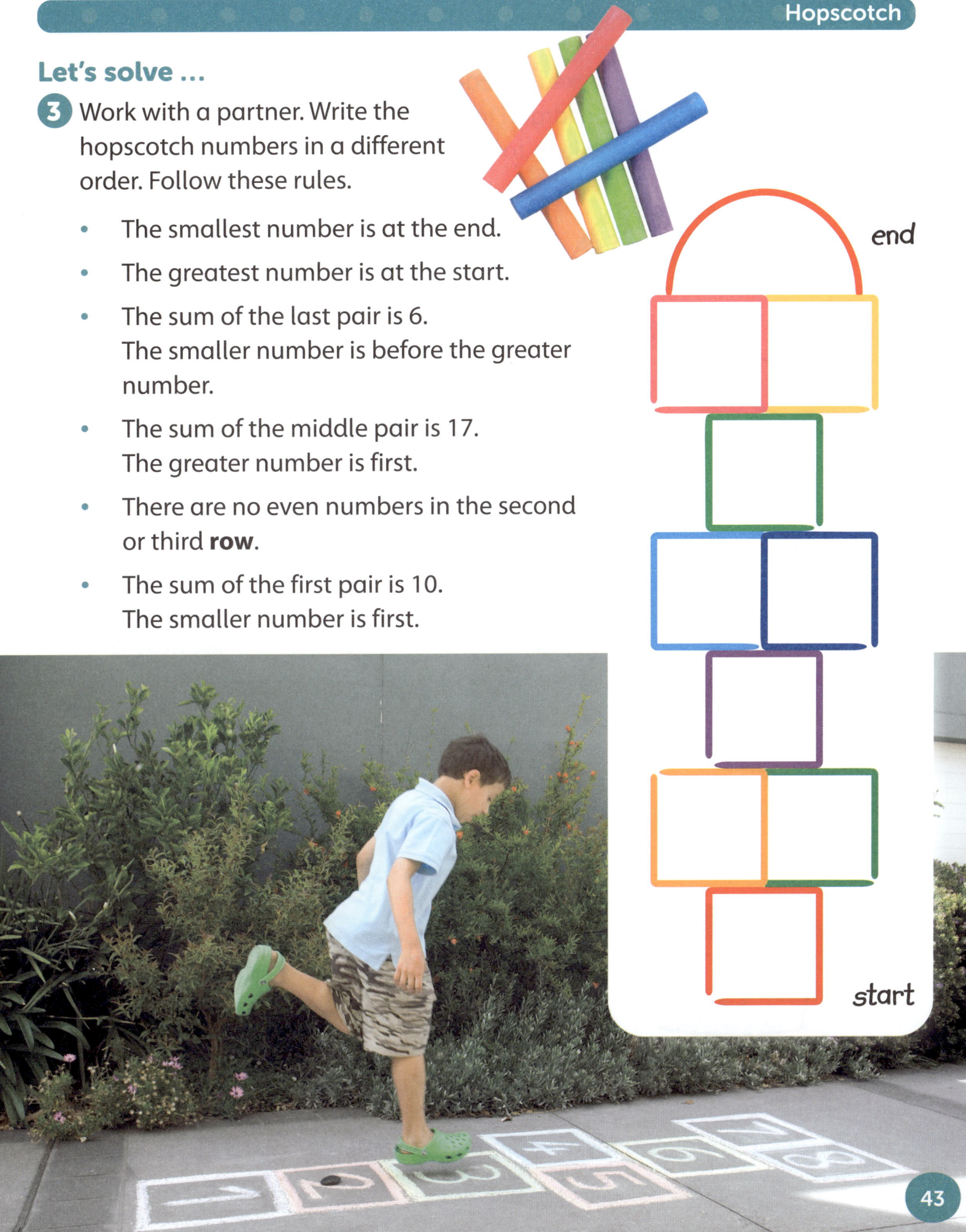

end

start

1 The sports equipment is mixed up. Each type of equipment has 3 sizes: small, medium and large. Find the matching sets. Then draw a line to match each item to the correct box.

2 Each type of equipment comes in 3 sizes.

How many different types of equipment do you see?

You can sort in different ways. In question 1, you **sorted** by size. You can also **sort** by shape, colour or type.

3 The circled item does not belong in the set. Why not? Write a word from the box in each sentence.

When we sort objects, we make groups that belong together.

| colour | shape | size | type |

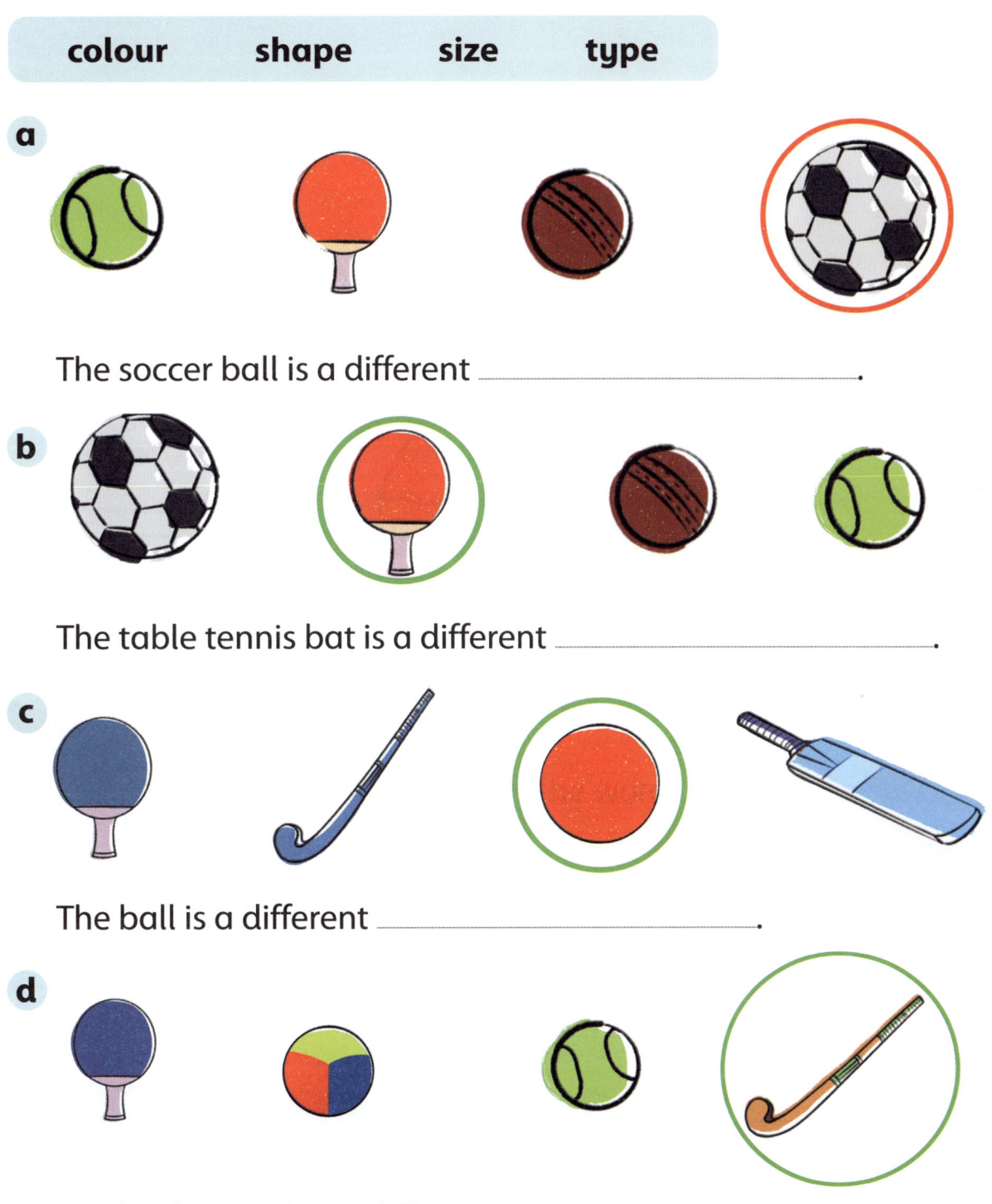

a

The soccer ball is a different _____.

b

The table tennis bat is a different _____.

c

The ball is a different _____.

d

The hockey stick is a different _____.

1 Each lunchbox has a snack, a fruit and a drink.

Read the clues. Draw a line to match each lunchbox to its fruit, snack and drink.

A **clue** is something that helps you to work out the information that you need.

My snack is long and straight. I have a drink in a box.

My fruit is crunchy. I have a snack in a square bag.

I have a yellow fruit. My drink is in a tall glass bottle.

spring roll

apple

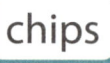
chips

juice

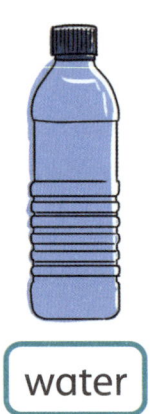
water

banana

grapes

milk

muffin

2 Each lunchbox has a different number of crackers. Read the clues and work out how many crackers are in each lunchbox. Write the numbers.

a

| The number of days in the week. | 1 more than the rainbow lunchbox. | 2 less crackers than the striped lunchbox. |

 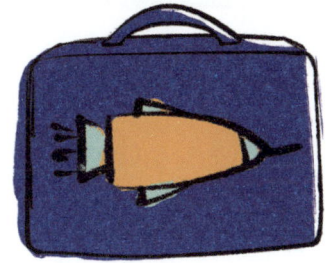 

b

| The number of corners on a square. | Double the number in the spotted lunchbox. | The total number of crackers in all three lunchboxes is 20. |

1 Complete the sentences about the students in the picture.

last   in front of   up   down   first   second

third   fourth   fifth   sixth   seventh   before

Luca is in _____ place. Tia is in _____ place.

The student in third place is _____.

Mira is in _____ place and Zayn is _____ Mira.

Luca is going _____ the slide.

The other students must go _____ the steps before they can

come _____ the slide.

2 Choose two of the words you did not use. Write your own sentences about the picture using these words.

_____

_____

Let's solve ...

3 When Luca gets to the bottom of the slide, he goes to the back of the line.

> You can act it out or draw a picture to help you solve the problem.

   a Who is in first place now? _____

   b Who is in third place now? _____

4 Complete the sentences.

When Jon is in first place, Luca is in _____ place.

There are _____ students between Jon and Luca.

5 This is a very tall slide. It has 14 steps.

   a Luca goes 8 steps up the slide. How many more steps are there to the top?

   _____

   b Luca goes up 2 more steps, then comes down 5 steps. Now how many more steps are there to the top?

   _____

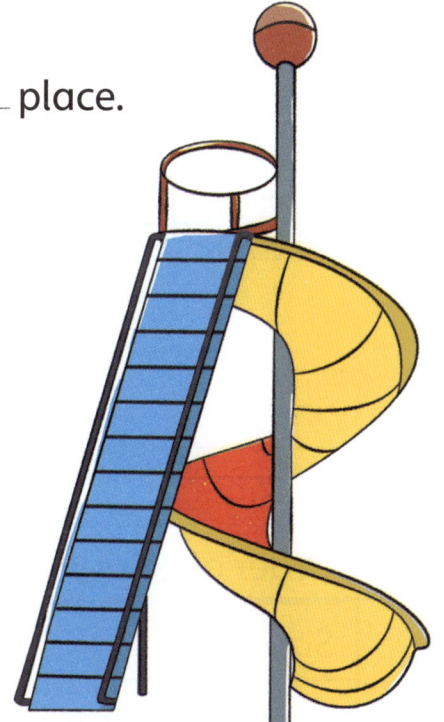

Fidget toys can help you to concentrate. Some fidget toys can help you to solve maths problems too.

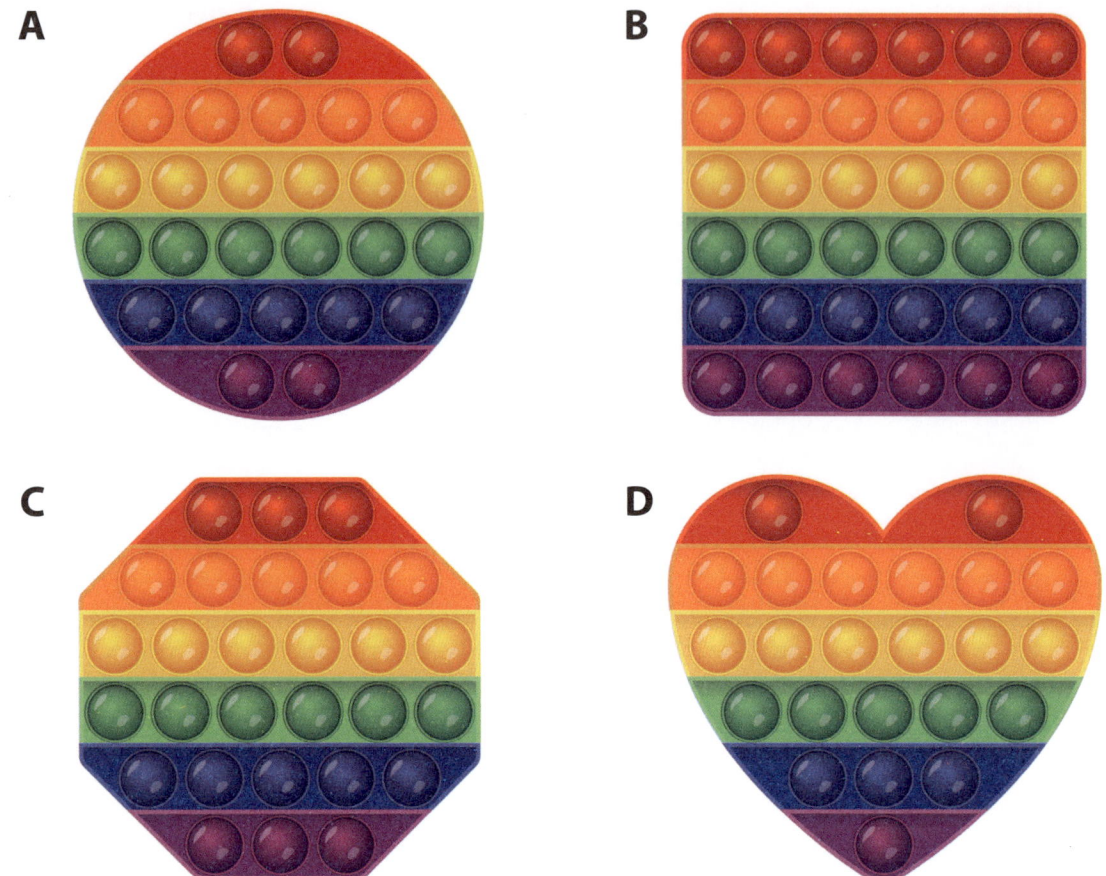

1 Look at the four fidget toys. What is the same and what is different?

Tick ✓ same or different for each row in the table.

	Same	Different
Shape		
Number of colours		
Order of colours		
Size		
Number of dots in the top and bottom row of the shape		

2 **Estimate** the answers to these questions. Do not count the dots.

   a Which fidget toy has the most dots? _____

       Estimate means guess.

       Which fidget toy has the fewest dots? _____

   b Tell a partner how you estimated.

3 Talk with a partner. How can you work out the number of dots on each fidget toy? You must not count all the dots. Write or draw your ideas here.

A	B
C	D

4 Use your ideas to work out the number of dots.

   A _____   B _____   C _____   D _____

5 Compare answers with another pair. Tick ✓ the boxes to answer the questions.

- Did the other pair find the same totals?   Yes ☐ No ☐

- Did they use the same way to find each total?   Yes ☐ No ☐

Count to check each other's answers. Then share your ideas.

A grid can help you to see what information you already have and what is still missing. It can also help you to make **connections**.

1 Gia, Ravi and Kareem ran in a race. They are all different ages.

a Use the grid to work out each student's age and their position in the race.

Clues:

The oldest student finished third.

Gia finished before Ravi and after Kareem

Kareem is older than Gia.

When you tick a box, you can shade out the other boxes in that row and **column**.

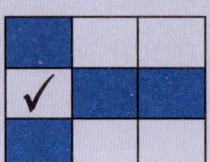

		Age			Position		
		5	6	7	First	Second	Third
Name	Gia						
	Ravi						
	Kareem						
Position	First						
	Second						
	Third						

b Who wins each trophy? Write the name and age.

 Age: ☐

 Age: ☐

 Age: ☐

Name: _____

Name: _____

Name: _____

2 Three students took turns to bounce a ball. They timed how long before each student dropped the ball.

a Use the grid to work out each student's time and which ball they bounced.

Clues:

Evan bounced the silver ball.

The student with the red ball bounced it for 2 minutes.

Sri's time was shortest.

		Time in minutes			Colour ball		
		1	$1\frac{1}{2}$	2	Silver	Black	Red
Name	Romy						
	Sri						
	Evan						
Colour ball	Silver						
	Black						
	Red						

b Complete the sentences.

• Romy bounced the _____ ball for _____ minutes.

• Sri bounced the _____ ball for _____ minute.

• Evan bounced the _____ ball for _____ minutes.

→ Turn back to page 4 and complete the problem-solving record.

Let's reason …

1 Count the eggs on each leaf.
Use the information to work out
how many will hatch.

You can circle groups
to help you count.

Ladybird A laid _____ eggs.

7 eggs do not hatch.

_____ eggs hatch.

Ladybird B laid _____ eggs.

6 eggs do not hatch.

_____ eggs hatch.

2 Newly hatched baby ladybirds are called larvae.
Julia put the larvae from ladybirds A and B together in a
container. How many larvae are in Julia's container? Draw to
work it out.

3 There are many kinds of ladybirds. Julia finds these 8 ladybirds.
She counts the spots to sort the ladybirds.
Write the letter of each ladybird in the correct box in the table.

Total number of spots	1 to 5 spots	6 to 12 spots	13 to 20 spots	21 spots or more
Ladybird				

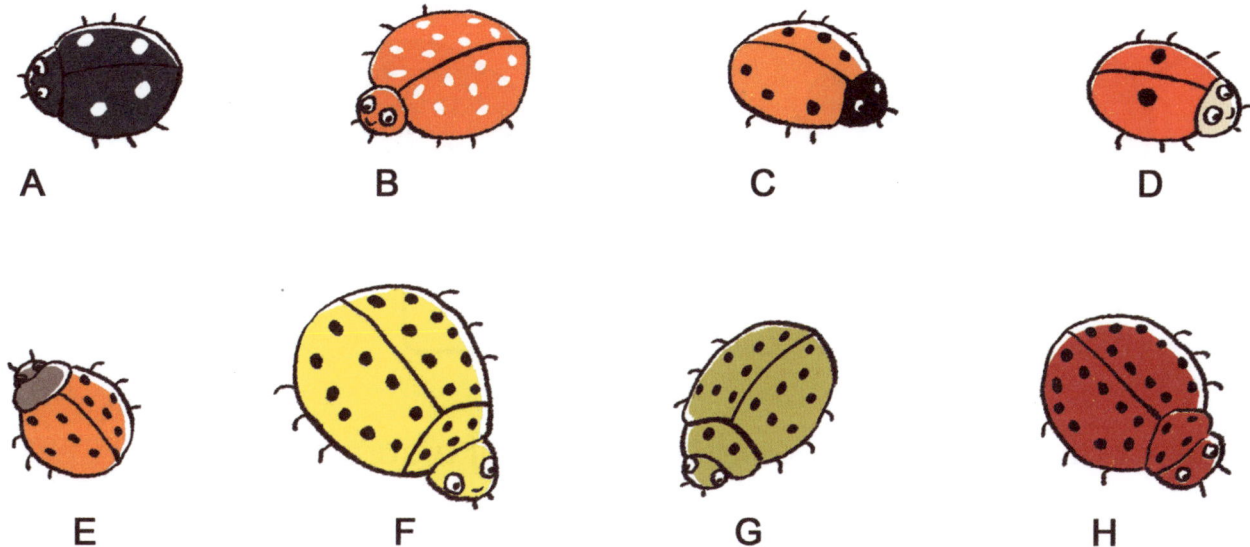

A   B   C   D

E   F   G   H

4 Miles finds 8 ladybirds that all have the same number of spots.
They have an equal number of spots on each wing. He counts
32 spots altogether.
Work with a partner. How many spots are there on each wing?
Use drawing to help you.

There are _____ spots on each wing.

Think, talk, write

Some insects eat guava leaves, mulberry leaves and fig leaves.

A  B  C

guava leaf   mulberry leaf   fig leaf

1 What kind of leaf is it? Write A, B or C below each leaf.

a   b   c   d   e   f

☐   ☐   ☐   ☐   ☐   ☐

2 One insect ate about $\frac{1}{2}$ a fig leaf and about $\frac{1}{4}$ of a guava leaf.

   a What does 'about' mean? Tell a partner.

   b Shade the part of each leaf that the insect ate.

3 Julia found these leaves. How much did the insects eat? Draw lines to match the fractions with the leaves.

The missing part shows you how much the insects ate.

about $\frac{1}{2}$ about $\frac{1}{4}$ about $\frac{3}{4}$

a

b

c

d

e

f

4 This is a block diagram to show how much the insects ate of each kind of leaf.
Use shading to complete the block diagram.

How much did the insects eat?

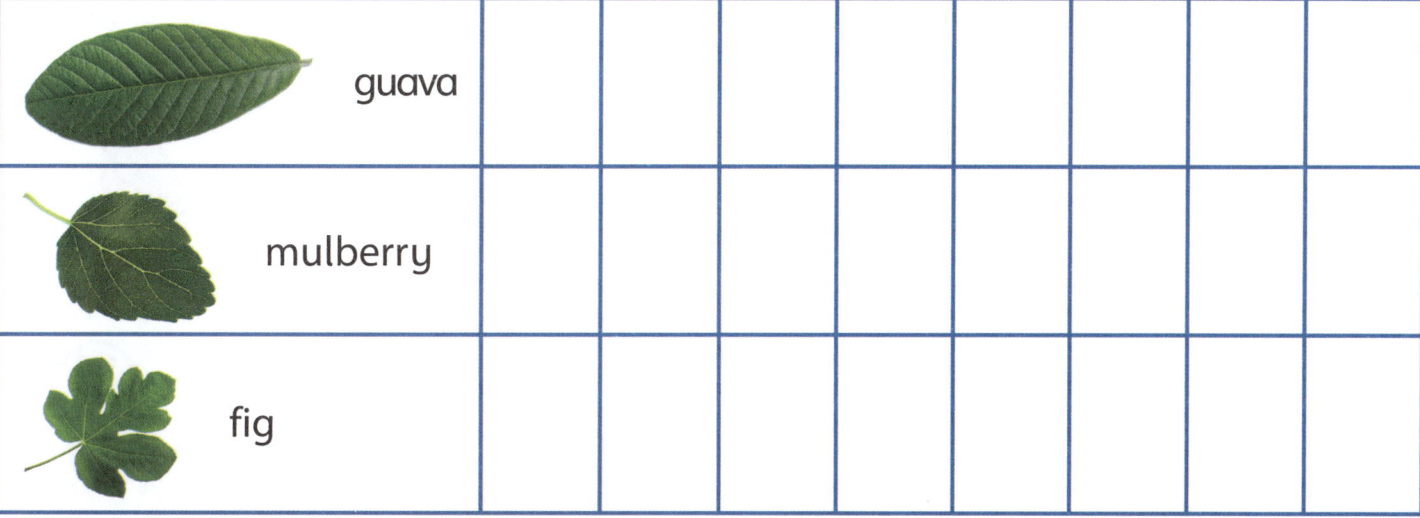

guava									
mulberry									
fig									

Key: 1 block = $\frac{1}{4}$ of a leaf

Let's reason …

These butterflies have **symmetry**.
Each side looks the same as
the other, like a **mirror image**.

1 Circle the matching wing to complete each pair of wings.

a

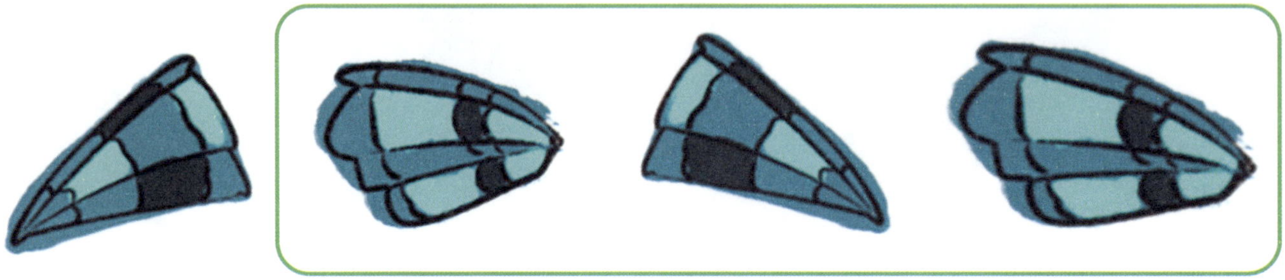

b

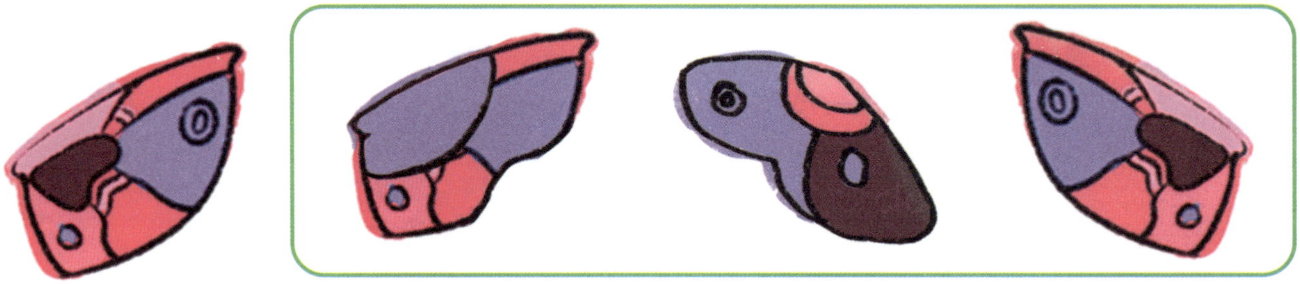

c

d

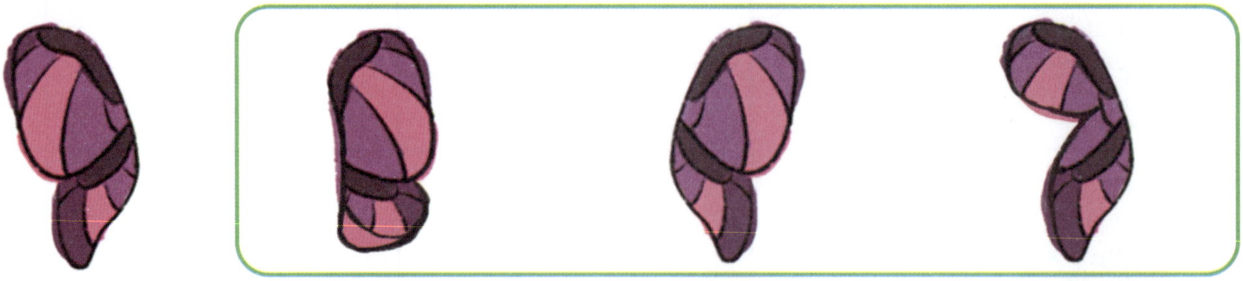

e

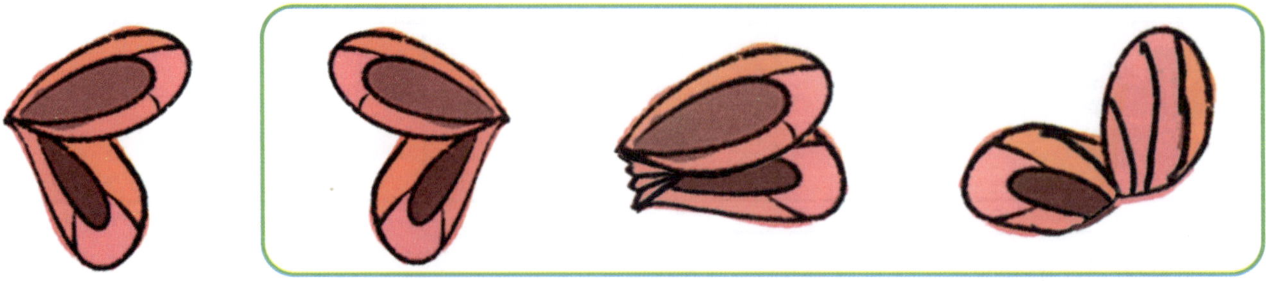

58

2 Draw the other **half** of this butterfly.

3 Draw your own symmetrical butterfly. You can use the grid to help you make your butterfly symmetrical.

Let's solve ...

A centipede has a pair of legs on each segment of its body.

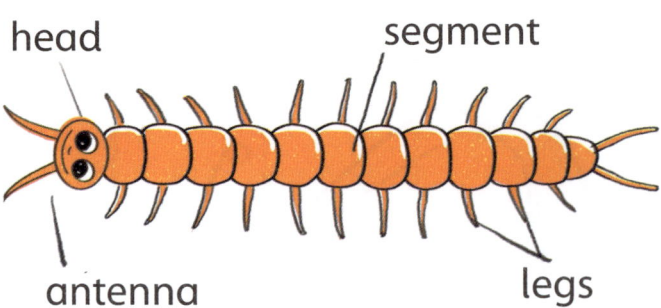

head   segment

antenna   legs

1 Centipede A has 16 segments.

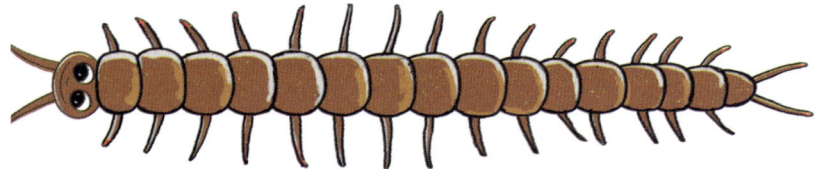

How many pairs of legs? _____ pairs

How many legs altogether? _____ legs

2 Centipede B has 4 more segments than Centipede A.

How many pairs of legs? _____ pairs

How many legs altogether? _____ legs

> Draw a picture to work it out.

3 Centipede C and Centipede D have the same number of segments. They have 100 legs altogether.

  a Circle the correct answer.

   Each centipede has 100 / 25 / 50 segments.

  b Tell a partner how you worked it out.

A millipede has 2 pairs of legs on each segment.

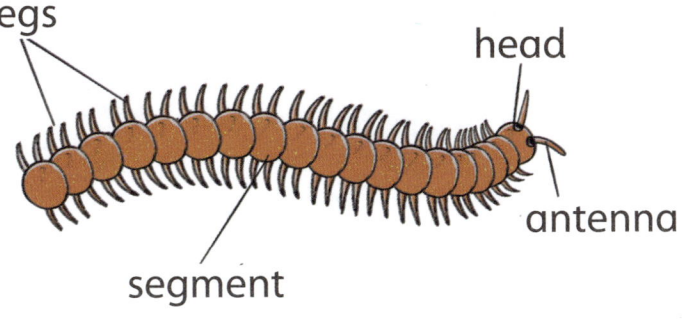

Remember,
1 pair is 2 legs.

4 Draw legs on the millipede.

5 a Complete the table.

Number of segments	1	2	3	4	5	6	7	8
Number of pairs of legs	2	4	6					
Total number of legs	4	8	12					

b Complete the statements using the words double or half.

- The number of pairs is _____ the number of segments.

- The total number of legs is _____ the number of pairs.

- The number of pairs is _____ the total number of legs.

6 In real life, millipedes have more segments.

a Circle the correct answer.

A millipede with 25 segments has   250   /   50   /   100   legs.

b Tell a partner how you worked it out.

Think, talk, write

A human begins life as a baby. Then you grow into a child, then an adult. These are the **stages** in your **life cycle**. This diagram shows the stages in a butterfly's life cycle.

eggs

caterpillar

Butterfly life cycle

butterfly

chrysalis

1 Choose the correct answer. Trace the word. Work with a partner.

a A butterfly begins life as a baby / a caterpillar / an egg.

b The caterpillar comes out of the chrysalis / butterfly / egg.

c The butterfly comes out of the chrysalis / caterpillar / egg.

d The adult animal is called a chrysalis / butterfly / larva.

2 Put the pictures in order. Write the letters in the table.

A

B

C

D

A butterfly's life cycle

first	next	then	last

Let's solve …

3 Read the clues. Match each butterfly to its leaf.

> The biggest butterfly laid the fewest eggs.

> The smallest butterfly laid an odd number of eggs.

 4 Gina counted butterflies in her garden every day. Read the clues and complete the diagram.

Shade 1 block for each butterfly Gina found each day.

> Gina counted 25 butterflies in total.

> There were no butterflies on the first or last day of the week.

> On Thursday there were double the number of butterflies on Wednesday.

> Gina counted 7 butterflies on Tuesday.

> Start with the clue that tells you the number for one day. Draw lines through the blocks for days with no butterflies.

> Use objects or drawings to help you work it out.

Monday											
Tuesday											
Wednesday											
Thursday											
Friday											

Think, talk, write

These bugs are on a grid. In this grid, each column has a letter and each row has a number.

1 **a** Row 2 has no bugs.

Which other row has no bugs?

row _____

b Column C has no bugs.

Which other column has no bugs?

column _____

7		🐌				
6						
5					🐝	
4	🐛					
3		🐞				
2						
1						🦋
	A	B	C	D	E	F

↑ up   ↓ down

← left   → right

2 Circle the correct word to complete each sentence.

a The ladybird must go up / down / left / right to get to the snail.

b The bee / caterpillar / snail / butterfly is closest to the ladybird.

3 The ladybird wants to get to the bee. Here is one way: up 2 blocks, right 3 blocks. Find another way.

4 Draw four small bugs on this grid. Make up three questions for a partner to answer about your grid. Swap with a partner and answer each other's questions.

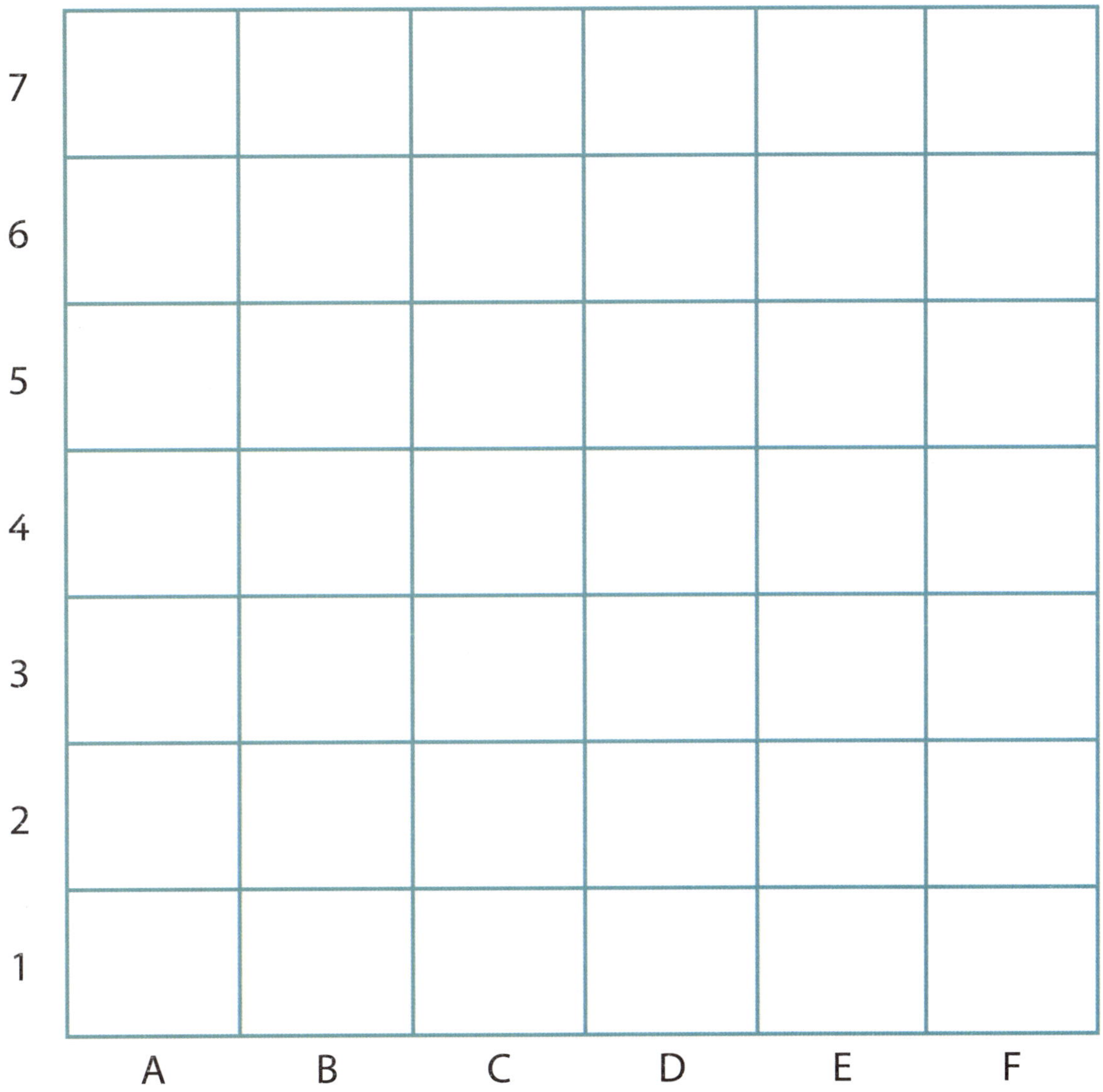

	A	B	C	D	E	F
7						
6						
5						
4						
3						
2						
1						

My questions:

_____

_____

_____

 Turn back to page 4 and complete the problem-solving record.

1 Which line did each pencil, pen or paintbrush make? Draw lines to match them.

thin   thick   medium   wide   long   short

2 Draw lines to match the words to the lines.

Each word may match more than one line.

3 Use your own crayons or pens to make a line in each box.

Make sure your line is the correct length and thickness.

		Length		
		Shorter	**Medium**	**Longer**
Thickness	**Very thin**			
	Medium			
	Very thick			

Ella's class does finger painting.
They use this design to paint pineapples.

1 How many fingerprints are in 1 pineapple?

_____

2 These students did not finish their pineapples.
How many more fingerprints does each student need?
Complete the instructions.

Each pineapple must match the design. How many fingerprints are missing?

a Paint _____ more fingerprints.

b Paint _____ more fingerprints.

c Paint _____ more fingerprints.

d Paint _____ more fingerprints.

3 These students made flower patterns with their fingerprints.
How many flowers did each student make?

I used 20 fingerprints altogether.

a I made _____ flowers.

I used 24 fingerprints altogether.

b I made _____ flowers.

I used 21 fingerprints altogether.

c I made _____ flowers.

You can draw people and animals using lines and shapes.

1 Timur drew these stick figures.
   Match each stick figure to the description.

2 circles,
no triangles

1 circle,
more then 10 lines

5 circles, 5 lines

1 circle, fewer
than 10 lines

2 circles,
1 triangle, 4 lines

1 circle, 1 triangle,
5 straight lines

2 Draw your own stick figures that have:

a more than 1 circle.

b 1 circle and 2 triangles.

Think, talk, write

3 Work with a partner. Look at these stick figures. What is the rule for the numbers in the circles? Write the missing numbers.

Rule:

Start with the stick figure that has all its numbers. Can you work out the rule for this stick figure? Check if the other stick figures follow the same rule. If the rule does not work, try again.

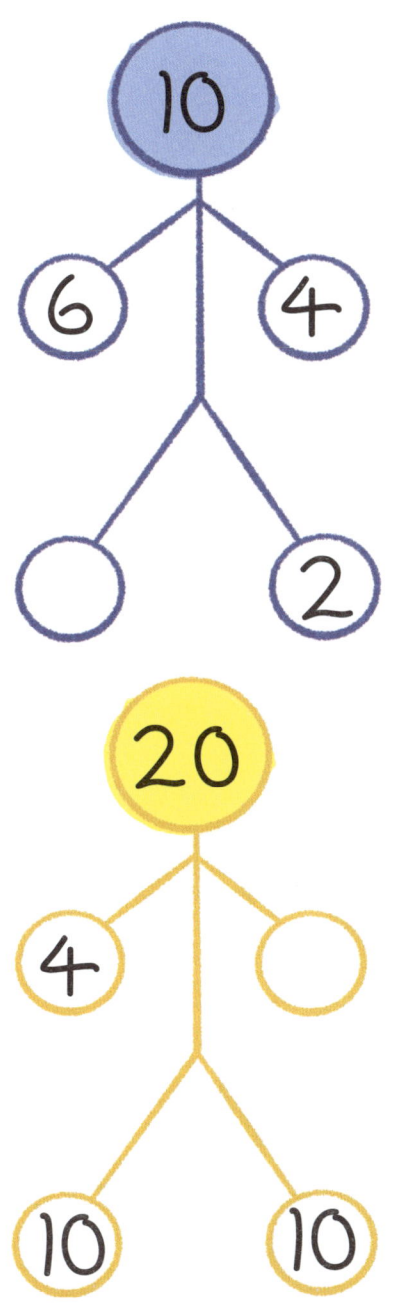

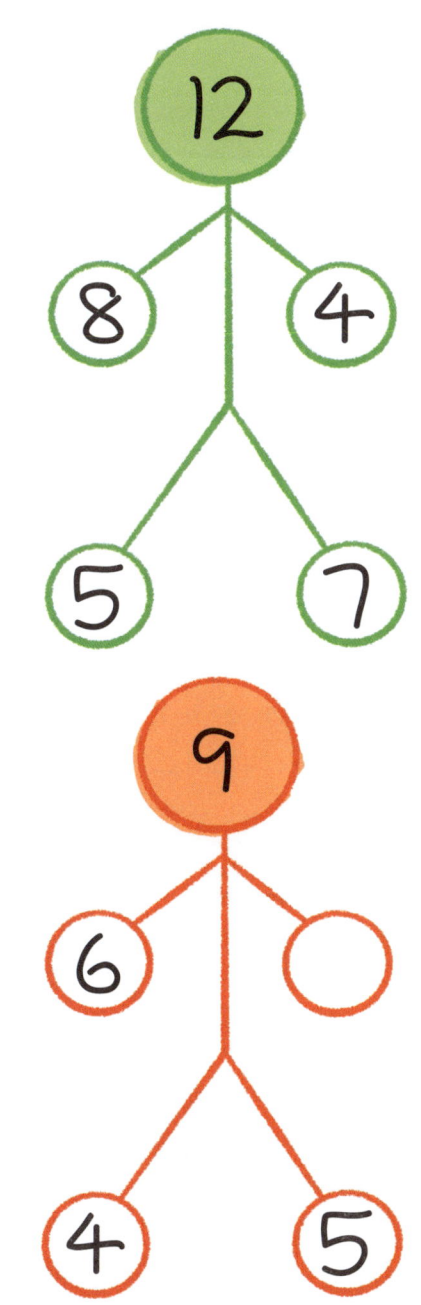

Bottles, buckets and jars are all kinds of containers.

An empty container does not contain any paint or water.

A full container contains all the paint or water that it can.

1 Where does each jar belong on the scale from empty to full?
Write the correct letter in each block.

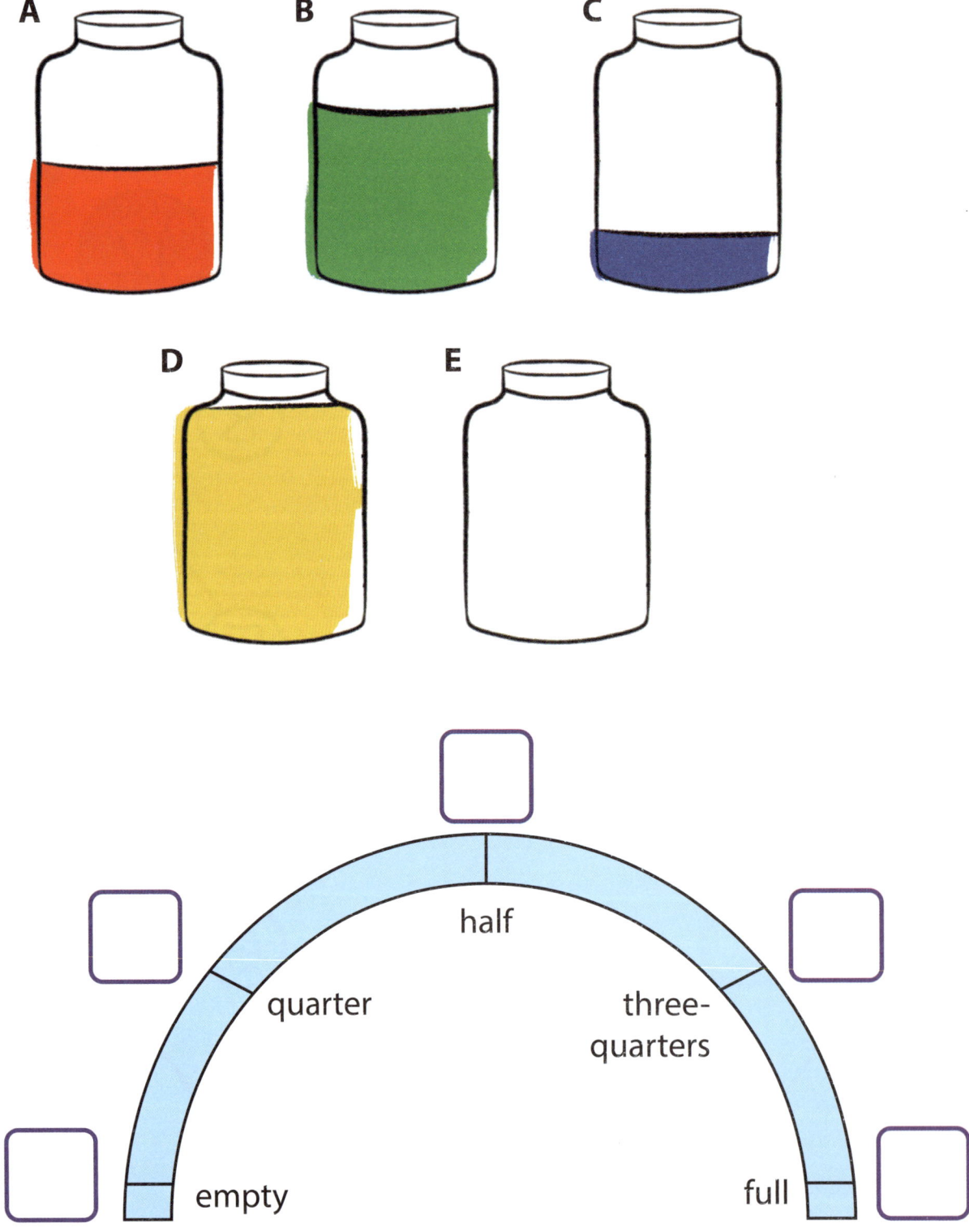

2 None of these jars are full.

a Work with a partner. Make as many full jars as possible. Draw arrows, lines or rings to make pairs or groups that equal a full jar.

b How many full jars are there now? _____

c How many jars are empty now? _____

d Are any of the jars not empty or full? Say why.

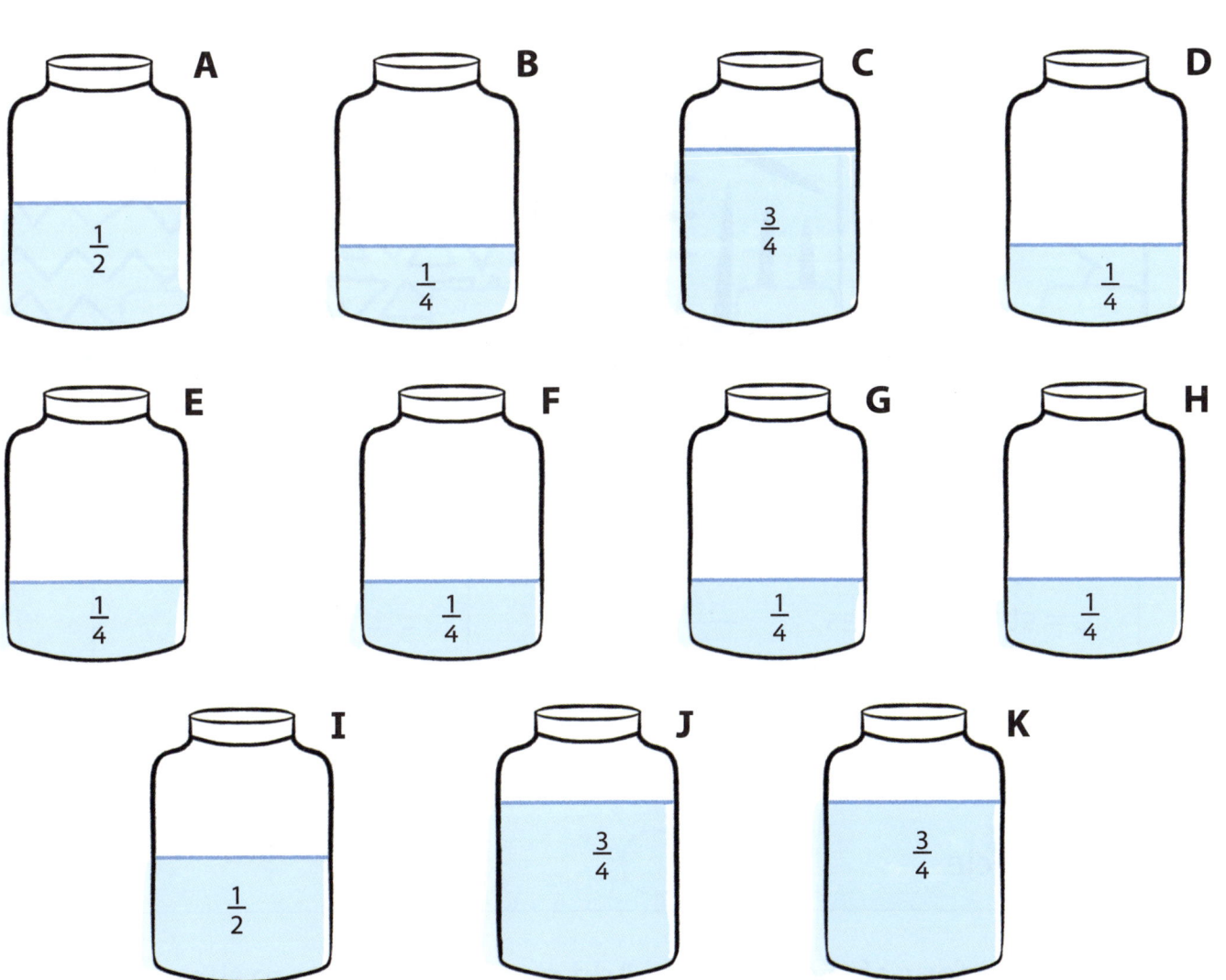

1 Look at the patterns in the grid.

a Each pattern was made mostly with one kind of line or shape.
Write the letter that best matches each pattern in the grid.

L = straight lines ——	S = square ☐
W = wavy lines ∿	R = rectangle ▭
Z = zigzag lines /\/\	T = triangle △
C = circle ○	

b Choose four of the patterns. Add a colour pattern to the shapes or lines.

2 Make different patterns in this grid that match the letters. In the last two blocks, choose a kind of shape or line. Write the letters and draw patterns to match.

W	L	C
Z	S	R
T		

lemon   onion   pepper   okra

1 Match each print to the fruit or vegetable that made it. Say or write the word.

A

B
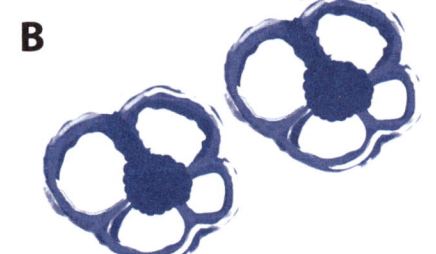

C
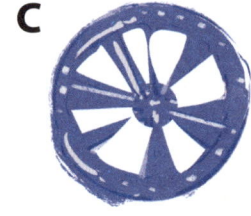

D

2 Read each clue. Write the fruit or vegetable.

I have many layers. When you peel away one layer, you find another layer underneath. My print has many circles inside each other.

I am a long, thin vegetable but my print looks like a small flower.

a _____

b _____

Let's reason…

3 Some students have used **3D shapes** to make prints. But some prints are in the wrong places. In each row, cross out the print that doesn't belong.

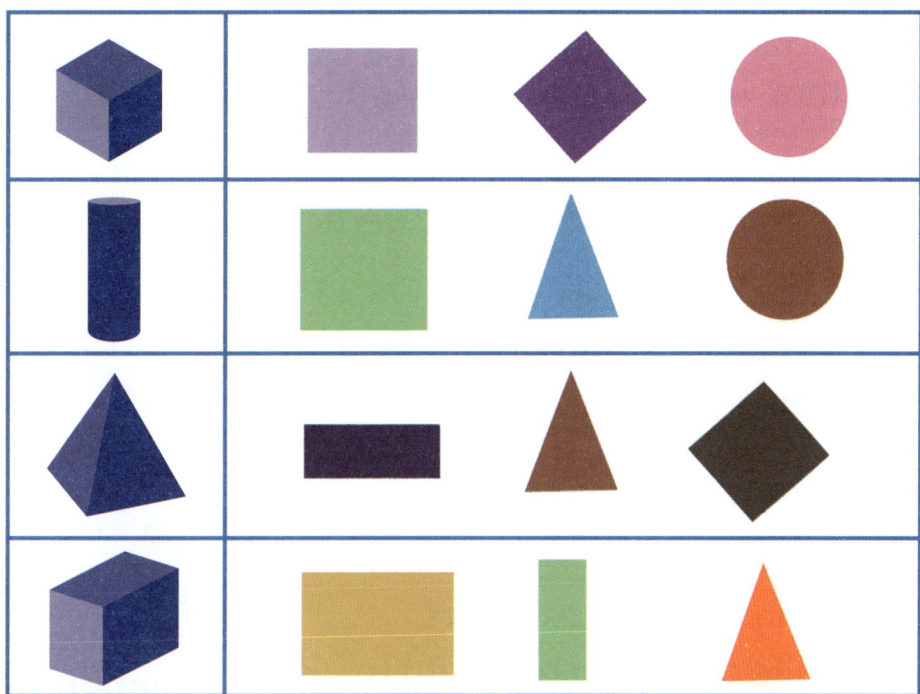

4 What kind of print does it make? Tick ✓ the correct column.

Object	Solid circle ●	Circle outline ○

Glossary

General terms

altogether in total; what you have when two or more amounts are added

clue a hint; something that will help you to solve a problem

column a vertical line, or objects arranged in a vertical line

data information that is collected, usually made up of numbers or measurements

grid rows and columns of equal-sized rectangle

information facts about something

life cycle how a living thing changes as it gets older, for example, the life cycle of a butterfly is: egg > caterpillar > chrysalis > butterfly

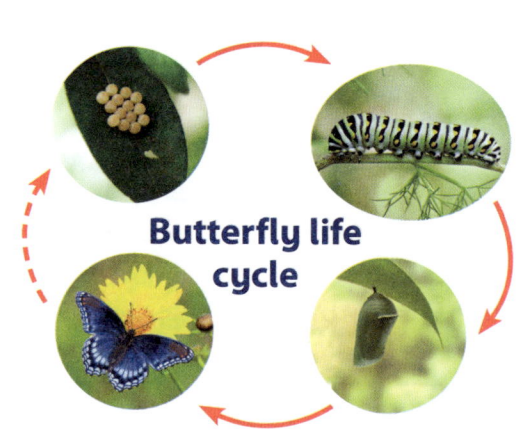

Butterfly life cycle

plan something that you set out to do

popular when something is liked by lots of people

position the location of something; where something is compared to other things

row a horizontal line, or objects arranged in a horizontal line

sort/sorted to arrange items in groups that share a common characteristic or property, for example to sort shapes by size or by colour

stage a period of time as something develops or grows, for example, the stages of a butterfly's life cycle are stage 1: egg, stage 2: caterpillar, stage 3: chrysalis, stage 4: butterfly

turn a rotation around a point either clockwise or anti-clockwise

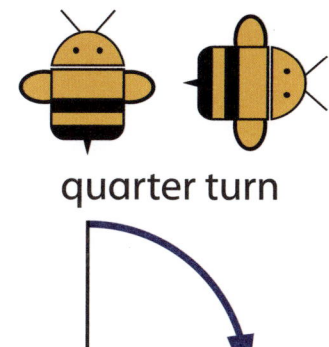

quarter turn

Mathematics terms

3D shape a shape that has three dimensions: length, width and height, for example, a cube or a cylinder

block diagram a type of chart made with blocks or rectangles to show how many there are of each thing

chart a diagram that shows information or data

diagram a way of showing information clearly using a picture

double two times an amount; twice as many

equal when two or more amounts have the same value

estimate a good guess, based on known information

half when an amount or an object is split into two equal parts, each part is a half

mirror image a reflection of an object, as if it is seen in a mirror

pair a group of two things

pictogram sometimes known as a pictograph) a chart or graph that uses pictures to represent data

share to divide an amount or set of objects fairly into equal groups

sum the total you get when you add two or more numbers

symmetry a mirror image, for example, a shape has symmetry if one half is a mirror image of the other half

79